Joyce Landorf Heatherley

The Inheritance

BALCONY PUBLISHING

AUSTIN, TEXAS 78734

THE INHERITANCE

Balcony Publishing Paperback Edition Published in 1989.

Library of Congress Cataloging-in-Publication Data:

Available

ISBN 0-929488-14-8

Scripture quotations in this publication are from the following sources:

The King James Version of the Bible (KJV).

The Living Letters (LL), copyright © 1962 by Tyndale House Publishers, Wheaton, Illinois.

The Living Bible; Paraphrased (TLB), copyright © 1971
by Tyndale House Publishers, Wheaton, Illinois.

The Revised Standard Version of the Bible (RSV), copyright 1946,
1952, © 1971 and 1973 by the Division of Christian Education
of the National Council of Churches of Christ in the U.S.A.

The Twentieth Century New Testament (TCNT),
Moody Bible Institute, Chicago, Illinois.

The Modern Language Bible: The New Berkley Version in
Modern English, copyright © 1945, 1959, 1969 by
Zondervan Publishing House, Grand Rapids, Michigan.

The New Testament in Modern English, copyright © 1958, 1959,
1960 by J. B. Phillips; the MacMillan Co., New York, N.Y.

Printed in the United States of America

This daughter lovingly dedicates this book to her mother,

Marion Uzon Miller

Mothers Day
May, 1966

My Dearest Mother,

I was thinking today of how poor we were while I was growing up but how rich you always were in ideas, creativeness and elbow grease! In those senses we were wealthy.

Remember my graduation formal? No money to buy one so you made it out of the dining room curtains!

Whatever it was we ever lacked in money you made up with a million ideas.

How precious you are to me—to all of us! We love you for the rich inheritance you've given us through the years! Keep it up!

Our love,

Joyce

Mothers Day
May, 1989

My Dearest Friends,

I am wise enough and definitely old enough to know that without your loving imprint on this manuscript, it would not have become a full fledged book.

So, from my heart, I thank you all! I am particularly mindful and beholden to;

Merikay Jones
Micheal Harper
Wendy Justice
Brenda Arnold
Celeste Heatherley Morgan
and Balcony Publishing.

You are loved by me,

Joyce

Mothers Day
May, 1989

My Dearest Daughter Laurie,

Bless your sensitive and tender heart for your inspiring words whispered to me after you heard my talk concerning the inheritance your grandmother left. I've held those words in my heart as I've written this manuscript.

I know, more than ever, that one of the loveliest gifts God ever gave me, was the unique privilege and honor of being your mother.

I love you Laurie-Honey.

My love,

Joyce

Chapter 1

Hello?

Hello, Joyce. This is your father.

Hi Daddy, how *are* you?

Oh, just fine . . . fine. . . . Say, by the way, Sunday I preached on Psalm 139. I know people would rather hear a sermon on the 23rd Psalm . . . but, oh my, there's so much *more* in the 139th . . . .

The phone conversation began exactly like hundreds I'd received in my life of being a "preacher's kid." Somewhere early on in each call Dad would give me (my sister, brother, or anyone else who would listen) a rehash of his latest sermon. After a Wednesday night prayer meeting and Bible study his call took on the same character. It was a part of our history with Dad, and it was understood that no new subject material would be interjected into the conversation until the sermon, with no lack of vigor, had been re-preached. No warmed over sermons for his children. They must be spoon fed the original! Some people hug each other by the warm tonal qualities in their voices over the phone, but my father—and I smile here as I recall the many times this was repeated—my dad, during each call, embraced me over those phone lines with his own life-long passion and love of preaching.

As Dad and I talked some things remained exactly as always, including a discussion of theological concepts and a general recapitulation or musical reprise of his last sermon. But lately, with each call, he was adding a significant request; and both of us would end up in a prickly stalemate of uncomfortable feelings.

1

As I write these memories out, it feels as if it happened only a brief heartbeat ago, or maybe just yesterday . . . It really was a long time ago. Yet, with vivid clarity, I remember November 12, 1966. That day when the phone rang, I thought, "Oh dear, that's Daddy . . . the third call from him this week." Emotionally, I cringed and tried to steel myself against the inevitable course his words would take . . .

Hello?

Hello, Joyce . . . how are you?

Fine, Daddy, just fine . . . you?

Oh, all right . . . I'm doing all right.

How's Marilyn doing in school, Dad? And, what do you hear from Cliff?

Oh, . . . let's see . . . Marilyn is at school . . . fine . . . fine . . . . I make breakfast every morning and get her off . . . Oh, and I made Irish stew for supper tonight. (I thought, *Again! My sister must be deathly sick of the only thing Dad seemed comfortable whipping up in the kitchen.*) I haven't heard anything from Vietnam, but I guess, from the TV news . . . Cliff is in the thick of it over there.

I miss him, Dad.

Yes, yes. I do, too. Vi Black baked one of her delicious cakes for us . . . and someone asked me at church Sunday the kind of pie I'd like to have . . .

Ah ha! And you said, "I'm particular. I only like *two* kinds of pie!" And after they stood there a moment, you did your line about . . . "Hot or cold."

That's right. Say, did I tell you what I preached about Sunday?

Yes, Dad, you did. It's a favorite of mine, "The Blue Ribbon." Remember, Daddy, how you'd offer a New Testament as a prize to the kid who took the best notes of "The Blue Ribbon" sermon? And I always won!

That's right . . . it was at the Lincoln Park Church in Michigan. You were about ten years old.

2

Yes, and I still remember that sermon. You told about the woman who had been sick for twelve years, pushing through the crowds just to touch the priestly blue ribbon around Jesus' tunic—believing, in faith, that if she could touch even the hem of his robe, she would be healed . . . I always won those contests, and you always awarded a New Testament. I remember fervently wishing that next time I won the prize would be a great looking sweater or a pair of those fuzzy angora bobby socks. Of course, it never happened.

Dad was chuckling about all the New Testaments I'd collected during my childhood when suddenly he stopped and fell silent. I knew the moment had come when he remembered his own purpose for calling. It was the only *real* thing on his mind those days.

His next words stretched across the phone lines like a blind man's hand grasping for something familiar in a strange place.

Joyce? . . .

Yes, Daddy.

Joyce, I need to talk to you about your Mother's things.

So much was wrapped up in the painful package of those two words—"Mother's things." Oh, God, the grief, the loneliness, the void left in our family, the unfathomable loss caused by her death . . . .

Joyce, I wish you'd come over and take care of Mother's things . . .

Okay, Daddy, I will soon . . .

No. You have to come today . . . Mother's things need to be boxed up, put away, or something . . . .

Today?

Yes.

But, Daddy, Reseda is seventy-five miles from Pomona, and it's already noon . . . .

I know . . . but tomorrow?

Okay, tomorrow.

I would have put the task off forever if I'd had my way. I was in no hurry to go to my parents' home knowing that the vibrant, sparkling centerpiece of the home was gone.

The drive west from Pomona, in the San Gabriel Valley, to the rustic city of Reseda, in the San Fernando Valley, is a distance I could drive blind-folded and, if pressed for time, could cover in just a little over an hour. But it was a trip I'd dreaded from a few days after my mother's funeral.

Mechanically, the next day I aimed my car onto the San Bernardino Freeway and (uncharacteristically for me) stayed in the slowest lane, gaining time to steel my emotions. What comes to memory about the drive to my parents' house was the running conversation I had with myself, even aloud, at points. I puzzled over the rush of intense memories and tried to calm the feelings flooding my thoughts.

Why does Dad insist that I do this? Why doesn't *he* do it? Why all the pushing and pressuring? Why do I feel not just prodded but literally shoved?!

Why can't he just let me heal and grieve at my own pace . . . my own speed?

I'm not ready to deal with this yet . . .

Why does he always want it done *now*?

Why can't it be put off until after Thanksgiving or Christmas? Another month or two isn't going to make *that* much difference.

By the time I was threading my way through the Los Angeles Civic Center interchange, I recognized the spring-head of my heart's feelings. I came to grips with the core of my problem: It centered on the two words of my father's calls which pained me the most . . . the words, *"Mother's things."*

4

My vivacious mother, Marion Uzon Miller, in her fifties, an extraordinary blend of intelligence, spirituality and compassion, ahead of her time, my dearest and very best friend, my balcony person (and occasionally my *sole* balcony person) had done the absolutely unthinkable, unbelievable thing. She had died.

Besides that, while she was in the process of dying, she did what some of those who "know" they are leaving often do. That is, they select just one member of their family or one special person whom they trust to wait *with* them. Someone who will be there during the difficult, confusing, and infinitely painful agony of the last days, weeks, and months.

Mother could have chosen my father, for of course, he was there. But along with being completely preoccupied with his struggling little church and the constant needs of the people of his congregation, the thought of Marion dying of breast cancer was just not thinkable. After all, they were about to celebrate thirty-eight years of marriage, three children, and the teamwork of pioneering four or five churches together. There wasn't any way Marion, he reasoned, would die so young or before he did. So Dad chose the camouflage of the den of denial, telling his family and the people of his congregation, a short time before her death, "All Marion needs is some rest and Grandma Uzon's chicken soup." And, with those words, he locked the door of death's affirmation firmly behind him. My father was not able to come out of that dark cave until two weeks after her funeral.

But for the fact that he was overseas during the last year of her life, my mother could have chosen my brother Cliff to be with her those last days. Cliff was a Marine corpsman, searching and finding the wounded and the dead in mined rice paddies, swamps, ancient French forts and small deadly hills and ridges of Vietnam. Daily, he with God's help, wrought heroic medical miracles which he chose to describe later, with a shrug of his shoulder, as routine, ordinary, and merely the job for which he was trained. Near the end of my mother's life the Red Cross contacted

5

him by radio, in one of those bloody killing places, and flew him home directly from the field, his fatigues and boots still splattered and caked with the red mud of Vietnam.

There was also, Marilyn Celeste, my twenty-years-younger sister, my parents' late-in-life child. She was tender and sensitive, but only fourteen years old. Mother knew that the "hospital policy" (a term most people come to hate during any extended stay at any hospital) stated clearly that visitors had to be sixteen or older.

A few days after Mother was admitted to the hospital, when she sensed that she would probably never leave, and that indeed this was her time to die—she did something she was good at. She assessed the situation as best as she could, thought it all through, and made some tough, yet sensible decisions. She gave her husband the freedom to go on with his lifetime commitment to the Lord and to his work with the people of his church. She knew her twenty-one-year-old son, Cliff, was in Vietnam, so that was that. She also understood that Marilyn was young and needed the daily routine of going to school and being at home to balance and maintain some sort of normalcy in her life. For these reasons, my mother chose me, the eldest of her children, to wait with her.

I began my vigil and was at her bedside constantly once she clearly understood God's timing about her own death. In almost all of the seven weeks she was in the hospital, I lived, ate and slept in her room. I took notes—mainly because she handed me a yellow tablet of lined paper like the one I'm writing on now, four new ball point pens (because she knew typewriters were my natural enemy), and said cheerfully, "Here, take notes." Looking back at that time, it was my introduction to learning firsthand about a curious phenomenon I could not label then but now have chosen to call "Bridges of Grace." For during those days I could almost see God building those sometimes plain and other times ornate bridges of grace for his child, my mother, during her transition journey from the Earthland to his presence in the homeland.

6

But now, coming into view and shunting aside my bereaved thoughts, was the green and white freeway sign, "Reseda Boulevard Next Exit." From somewhere deep within me I heaved an unbidden sigh and thought out loud, "I'm almost there . . . oh, God." Yesterday, I'd pleaded . . .

Dad, listen to me, I'm just not ready.

Oh, yes, Joyce . . . you can do it.

But, Dad, you don't understand . . . I can't just sort out and sack up *Mother's things*. It's not that simple.

She didn't have a lot of things.

I know. But I need more time, Daddy. Don't you remember that I was the one who was at UCLA Medical Center for all those weeks? Daddy, I was there night and day!

I know . . . but you've got to come.

But, Dad, it's time for me to catch up on things here at home. After Cliff went back to Vietnam, you and Marilyn had Aunt Ellen to hold you two together, and for a few weeks she put the house back into some kind of order . . . remember?

Yes, but . . .

Well, now, Daddy, I'm needed here. My husband feels neglected. Laurie and Rick are back at school, but they are having a hard time . . . they are terribly lonely for their grandma. Besides, I have a deadline to meet for my column in *King's Business* magazine and weeks of radio broadcasts to tape at KBBI for my program, and . . . .

I would have gone on and on with my reasons, my fears and my excuses for not going over to my parent's house. I still had countless convincing arguments left when it occurred to me that Dad had stopped talking. He was no longer interrupting me about coming over to take care of "Mother's things." I waited.

Dad, are you there?

Yes . . . .

7

Daddy, did you hear me? I'm needed at home.

Yes, I know . . . but . . . .

It was then as if his rich, resonant baritone voice, the one I so dearly loved to hear, left him. It dried up, went flat and lifeless. I could feel the crushing of his soul by the immense heaviness of his grief. I heard him over the phone, as he stammered and tried to communicate through the veil of his overwhelming loneliness.

You don't know, Joyce . . . you don't . . . understand, Joyce. You must come . . . I can't walk down the hall past the den . . . can't go in there. Please, I can't do it . . . can't . . . can't.

Off the freeway now and on the city streets I kept hearing the unfamiliar dead tone of my father's voice and his compelling request to take care of "Mother's things." With my emotions wildly gyrating—from the guilt of knowing I *should* be there taking care of her things to fervently wishing I was someplace else and dreading everything about the whole encounter—I made the appropriate turns and then one final right swerve into my parents' driveway. I had arrived. I was there . . . nothing to do but go in.

The house at 19016 Cantlay was not very large, but it had a charming ginger-bread cottage exterior, as did most of the houses in that subdivision, and my mother had worked her usual magic on each room inside the house. It was lovely, but being there, seeing it again, gave me the visceral feeling that my heart was being squeezed in a vise.

I sat in my car, staring at the house, taking it all in and trying to understand what was so different. The house, while the stucco walls were painted a light cream color and the shutters and trim were a soft French blue, had a dark, forbidding, almost sinister look. Most of all, though, there seemed to be an animate aura of grief shadowing the house. My heart was broken. Putting my head down on the

8

steering wheel for a few moments, death's disconsolate reality took my breath away.

Dad must have spent the morning watching for me because I had barely touched the front door when he opened it. He stood smiling nervously in the entrance and greeted me warmly. Yet, the stress and strain of his bereavement was written on his face. He didn't try to disguise his gratitude for my visit nor did I miss the obvious relief in the inflection of his voice when he patted my shoulder and said, "I'm glad you're here."

We had a few moments of small talk in the front hall and then he walked away. I could hear him puttering about in the kitchen but I didn't go after him. I understood that he had left so I would get on with my task of the day. All I wanted was to walk quietly through the house, looking and remembering, but I knew if I started a tour of memories I'd only be putting off what inevitably must be done. So, without giving the living room a glance, I waited for a bit until I felt the level of my courage was a little stronger than the depths of my reluctance. Then I walked in slow motion down the hall to the room in which my beloved mother had spent her last year.

The den was pretty much as she had left it. For a little while I stood looking, reflecting and surveying the room which was, in my mind, synonymous with my mother. Since she was a genuine card-holding librarian, it was no wonder that one whole wall was lined from floor to ceiling with bookcases crammed full of books. I smiled, remembering that I could never out-read her. Many times I'd bound into the den talking about some new book I'd just read, ending my enthusiastic endorsement with, "Mother, you've just got to read this book!" . . . only to see her smile, shake her head, point to the bookcase or the book in her hand and say, "Too late."

Beside the doorway where I was standing, the room had a short wall with a space for her sewing cabinet. On the wall in front of me was a window with a studio couch below it that opened up into a bed. The bed was gone now, all neatly tucked away inside the couch, leaving no trace of the extraordinary woman who had lain there for so long. The wide double doors to Mother's closet took up most of the space on one wall. It was the place in the room I wanted to avoid most, so I made a point of studying the circular braided rug on the floor which I had made and given to her. I never did quite figure out a way to make the center lie down—even though I'd gone to night school to learn the secrets of rug braiding. At least I could be smug about making it big enough. It did cover most of the hardwood floor; but, somehow in lacing it together, I'd never been able to get the unwieldy circles in the middle to nestle flat. I was always grateful that Mother pretended the bump in the center of the rug was meant to be and was a part of its handmade charm. Even after I had once completely relaced it, sewn it together again, and steam ironed it, she still failed to notice the great camel hump. It was clear that she just loved the idea that her daughter made and presented it as a Mother's Day present, and she wouldn't allow herself to be negative about the rug's quite obvious flaw.

I knew I should move into the room and start the task I'd come to do—but the small den was alive with memories begging to be examined and relived.

It was in this place, every afternoon, that Mother waited, with exuberant joy, for Marilyn to come home from school. My sister would eagerly climb onto the opened couch, right next to Mother, and lie down. The two of them would then spend the rest of the afternoon talking, reading all sorts of books and articles aloud, or just sharing ideas and dreams. The wonderful ambiance of learning pervaded during those precious times, and it moved me deeply as I stood in this dear, bittersweet place.

Praying for the manna of strength and determination, I managed to find some cardboard boxes. Taking a deep breath, I shut the den door behind me and pulled off my coat. Dropping my handbag on the couch, I took a firmer grip on my determination, walked stoically over to Mother's closet, and said, "Now!"

If you have ever been assigned the task of taking care of a special loved one's "things," then you know how I felt as I came face to face with those closet doors. It's rather like our ability to remember where we were and what we were doing at the time of President Kennedy's assassination. It's an icicle memory, frozen to the wall of the heart. One has only to mention a person's name or a moment in our history, and the memory is thawed. Uninvited tears streaming down our cheeks remind us that we remember more than we can bear to acknowledge. We never forget some things, or the feelings that went along with the memory, or where we were and what we were doing.

The closet had been shut since Mother's death. My Aunt Ellen had lovingly cleaned the room; and once I'd spent a few hours there with Mae Smith, grateful for her offer and help in writing thank you notes to the hundreds who had sent expressions of sympathy and compassion to our family. But, even then, the closet doors had remained closed.

I'll never forget the flood tide of emotions that morning as I pulled open those long sealed doors. Even now, so many years later, I still feel the surprise at the poignant catch in my chest and the wave of grief which washes over me with an intensity as fresh, and sobering as when I first turned those knobs.

The moment the doors were opened, I was wrapped in the scented cloak of my mother's perfume, White Shoulders. The intoxicating bouquet of her favorite scent floating around me created the eerie illusion that she was alive! She had come back. She was there, somewhere close by, clothing me with fragrance.

I've no trouble at all believing that at birth a baby's most highly developed sense is not that of taste, touch, sight or hearing, but it is the sense of smell. The effect of the White Shoulders was powerful and awesome.

For a second or two I half expected to see Mother come popping out between the clothes . . . as if we'd been playing the child's game of hide and seek and I'd just discovered her hiding place. I probably wouldn't have been too startled to hear her usual cheery "Yoo Hoo!" greeting from somewhere deep inside that closet. The fragrance instantly drew an intuitive portrait of her. I could see her marvelous high cheekbones, her smooth beautiful skin and her dark sparkling Hungarian brown eyes which took in more wonderful things than anyone else's . . . especially when she was looking at her children.

I buried my face in the soft folds of her dresses and, for as long as I could bear it, I breathed in the delicious intimate smell of her . . . and I cried. I cried for the raw emptiness her loss carved in my heart. I cried because I wanted my mother.

When she had gone to the hospital this last time she was merely carrying out a now familiar routine: Her lungs would fill with fluid from the cancer; the hospital procedure would require a few hours to drain them and then, in a couple of days, she would be home. She fully expected to go through the routine, come home and then pick up right where she left off. In her closet, her belongings—clothes, shoes, boxes of old jewelry, her sewing basket, embroidery threads, yardage, and patterns, and all her previously purchased gifts waiting for Christmas wrapping—were just as she had left them . . . except her plans and her trip to the hospital had been anything but routine.

Still pinned to her dresses or suit jackets were her various PTA pins. She had been appointed the inspirational advisor at the school for years. This was a tribute to her marvelous spirit—a fact that was dear to me because even though she was a Gentile and a pastor's wife, the predominantly Jewish women of their neighborhood always gave her the job of being their PTA's spiritual advisor. Mother had been dearly loved by the Jewish mothers of the school. I stood there beholding the collection of Mother's PTA pins and other service organization pins in my hand and realized they were tiny bright symbols which represented the true heart-core of her attitudes and responses to life. Now my tears were joy drops because my mother's life had been a light, a lamp unto the feet of all who had the gift of her presence.

12

Now I saw clearly, as never before, that my mother had been far more interested in serving others than in her own self- interests. The pins told the story. Her work as inspirational chairman in the PTA, the after school love-of-her-life with children in Christian Release Time, the endless Daily Vacation Bible Schools she organized and ran, the church youth choirs she directed, the Bible study classes she taught, and her dearly loved position as counselor for Lambda Theta Chi, a Christian sorority founded by Dale Evans Rogers—all of this was a part of her calling to serve and minister to others. Her mission field had once been a call to Africa, but that had not worked out, so anyone she met was her mission and any relationship her mission field. She chose to bind up the wounds of any bruised, battered and broken victim of cruel forces. Her whole ministry was definable by one word: Others.

The day before Mother had a biopsy on a lump in her breast, some three years before her death, she jotted down the Bible verse and her heart's cry of the moment in her journal. Apparently she had been reading Romans and had come to Paul's words,

And dear brothers, I plead with you to give your bodies to God. Let them be a living sacrifice, holy—the kind he would accept.

Romans 12:1, *Living Letters*

Typical of her writing style, the Romans 12:1 reference headed the page, along with the title, *"Body Presented."* Then came her musings on the ancient verse *and* on her present day thoughts. She had written,

Hand it over to the Lord for Him to live in it —the life that He pleases. Lord, You may do with me what You please. You may take this body and do with it as you desire. It is your body. I now present it to Thee and it's Yours from this moment on . . . Help Yourself to it.

13

Lord, I'm going in the hospital. I'm just a weak, unknown handmaiden of Thine—with no knowledge of what's ahead or of the acquaintance with hungry hearts I may meet there.

Here is my body—my hands, feet and lips. Take them and use them for some troubled, burdened hearts. Speak through my lips, Thy words of light and life.

How wonderful to know that God is mine, to feel that He dwells in my heart, rules my will, my affections, my desires, and to know that He loves me!

The next day she had no opportunity to write in her journal because her body suffered not just biopsy but radical mastectomy before lunch time.

Even the mere thought of a biopsy on *my* breast tends to move my emotions from calm to chaos. Yet, my mother's main concern was clearly not for herself but for others: People whom she might meet—nurses, patients, doctors, cleaning women . . . whoever was troubled or broken. She wanted God to use her body, her hands, feet, lips to comfort the broken hearted.

A few days after the surgery, while I was visiting her, a nurse beckoned me out into the hall and asked if she could speak with me a moment.

"I just wanted to tell you something . . . it was so funny . . . . Your mother was still in surgery when we began receiving all these flowers and plants for her. Everyone kept asking, 'Who *is* this Marion Miller? Is she an actress, a famous celebrity, or what?'"

I smiled to myself . . . the phrase "unknown handmaiden" came to mind.

"But," the nurse continued, "what I want to tell you is . . . *I* know who she is! Marion is the woman who saved my life the night of her surgery. I'll never forget her." Her voice trailed off, the tears started gathering, but she quickly checked them and regained her professional composure. Before the woman left me standing in the corridor she said, "I can't talk about what happened that night yet, but, believe me, I wouldn't be alive today if it weren't for her!"

All I could think was how in the world, in such a short time span, did my mother manage to work into her own surgery and recovery schedule the saving of someone's life?

Years later, as I recounted in *The Fragrance of Beauty*, I learned the graphic details of the nurse's story, Mother's encounter, and of the incredible emotional healing which had taken place that night. It wasn't surprising, not even a cause of astonishment. Mother took life changing encounters with people, brief or lengthy, as if they were perfectly normal and routine.

To her, it was simple. You give yourself, as in Romans 12:1, your *whole* self, to the Lord and you pray prayers such as,

> Here is my body, my hands, feet and lips. Take them and use them for some troubled, burdened hearts. Speak through my lips, Thy words of light and life.

Then, you keep a sharp lookout for the hurting people who (given the pain density on this planet) always come into your line of sight. It was no big deal that they might even come into your hospital room the night of your mastectomy surgery. Come they would—presenting you with the opportunity to minister in whatever way you could and to trust the beneficence of God to use your humble efforts. My dearest, darling Mother believed God would hear even a "weak, unknown handmaiden's" prayer and would speak through her lips to touch and heal the issues which were wreaking havoc in a person's life.

Whether Mother was feeling wonderfully well or was desperately ill, she was ever on the alert for the hurting person, ready to carry out her mission of *being* God's love to others. Many times when she was at a church meeting or a social gathering, I'd watch her enter a room, survey the people for a fraction of a second, and then make a bee line for one person. Nine times out of ten it was a wounded or heavy-hearted person who desperately needed another human being to hold them. To really *touch* them.

15

My sister, Marilyn Celeste Hontz, now a pastor's wife, remembers Mother's instructions about reaching out to others, even in the Sunday morning service. The words went something like this:

Now, Marilyn-Honey, when you become a pastor's wife, [from the age of two Marilyn had stated her firm plan to marry a minister] don't sit in the same seat each Sunday. Move around. Sit by someone who is alone. Someone who looks lonely. Someone who is shy or quiet. Don't sit in the middle of little groups of friends, but sit by someone who is hurting and needs a friend.

For a long time I thought her instant rapport with hurting people happened because God gave her the gift of discernment—sort of a spiritual crystal ball—but I think now it was much more. Mother seemed secure in the understanding that God *really* did *love* her. They were a team. Consequently, secure in that knowledge, she was unthreatened by the dreadful or shocking events and circumstances which occurred either in her life or in the lives of others. When someone poured out their agony, she listened without feeling the need to be the authority figure, the judge, or the jury. She left that part of the team effort to God. No sin was *too* ugly to be looked upon. No choice, action or failure *too* disgusting to handle, and no wound or scar was *too* raw or hideous to touch. She just listened and then plunged into the job to be done.

Of course, it was never *that* simple. Nothing is. But, I'll say this for her, Mother gave it all she had. And I don't care what anybody says . . . I *know* that when she walked into Heaven's courts on September 22, 1966, it was only seconds before someone grabbed her and said, "Oh, Marion, I'm so glad you're here. You don't remember me, but one Sunday morning at the Reseda Community Church I was at the end of my rope. I was all alone and felt like I was going insane. You came over to me and sat down. Then you just loved me."

16

It was as I was removing Mother's Lambda Theta Chi pin that my fingers slowed down my task again. It took the longest time before I could set it aside because I kept looking at the small Greek letters which meant, to all who wore it, that it was an emblem of service. I recalled my mother's love for those women and of their devotion to her. She had been a counselor's counselor, a teacher's teacher, and a one-woman support group to all of them.

In February, that year, Mother had dramatically blossomed and bloomed with rosy, radiant health. God, doctors, and chemotherapy gave her almost five months of an incredible cancer free remission. She felt and looked absolutely vibrant!!

Remission: such a miraculous word.

But, by June the chemotherapy simply stopped working. The fluid in her lungs and upper chest area began building at an alarmingly fast rate. Almost over night her arms and chest were swollen, the skin stretched and straining from the fluid pressure within.

Slowly and sadly, she realized the good times were almost over. But I think she also knew, and gratefully so, that the months had given her a precious commodity: time. As usual, she had used those pain-free months to talk, listen and share with family, friends and even strangers. The time also gave her the opportunity to put her house in order and to deal with some of the "unfinished business" we all have in our lives.

Because the Lambda pin in my hand was an emblem of service it reminded me that it represented one of the hardest decisions she had to make, a decision she put off longer than any other: that of resigning her position as counselor.

The executive committee had accepted her resignation reluctantly, and they promptly planned an evening to honor her, giving me the privilege of being the main speaker.

I'll always be grateful that we went together to her last meeting. The lovely home in the Hollywood Hills was filled with equally lovely, spiritually oriented women. I remember the awesome mix of emotions as I watched her. There

17

was joy while I sat looking at Mother's face as she accepted gifts and listened to accolades; but, at the same time, there was the gut-wrenching ache of knowing that soon she would be gone, and in my chest grief sank like a heavy stone. As the women continued to shower their beloved Marion with gifts (such as an elegant pair of white lounging pajamas) and eloquent tributes (at this moment a woman was reading a letter Mother had written to her at the time of her husband's death), I knew I had to get out of the room! I stumbled over several guests, trying not to crush toes and feet, but when I escaped to the kitchen, I fell completely apart, sobbing on a friend's shoulder.

"She's dying, Jean! She's dying . . . ."

Moments later someone came for me and took me back into the living room. It was time for my part of the program. I have no earthly idea of anything I said or how I even managed to make sounds emanate from my vocal chords . . . only the memory of seeing Mother sitting on a low ottoman in front of me, surrounded by a sea of faces, looking up at me with her dark sparkling eyes which seemed to shout, "Okay, Joyce-Honey, let's hear what wonderful things you have to share . . . ."

I lifted a couple of dresses off the clothing rack, out of her closet, and laid them on the couch to fold. As I was smoothing out the folds, I discovered wadded up facial tissues in her pockets. As it turned out there were facial tissues in every pocket of every dress, skirt, jacket, blouse or coat. The tissues struck me as a quaint mini-mystery. She hadn't had a cold in a year or two and, as far as I knew, she didn't have any allergies. So why this mountain of tissues in front of me? I was still trying to figure it out, even after I'd swept all of the white, pink and other rainbow colored wads of tissue into the wastepaper basket . . . when suddenly, I knew. The tissues had been wadded up and retained their hard, crumpled shapes because they had been soaked with Mother's tears.

I can't even guess how many people she saw or talked with that last year, but I know there were large numbers, a

18

multitude of friends and acquaintances. Everyone, even strangers, sensed, rather than "knew as a fact," that time with her was at a premium. She knew, too, that the kind of listening and counseling she'd always done was drawing to a close. So, whether in a lengthy counseling session, a brief chat, a letter, or a hurried phone conversation, there had been, that last year, the underlined *absence* of small talk. People, young and old, had not discussed the weather or even asked too much about her health but had gone straight to the pivotal issues of their lives. They told her the things which haunted them day and night . . . the brokenness of their relationships with God or with people . . . their shattered dreams and ruined plans . . . their unthinkable icy fears and hot resentments . . . their inner wishes to die which gnawed at them like an invisible cancer . . . . All of these emotional and spiritual states, and many more, were poured out of the deep recesses of the people who had encounters with Marion Miller that year.

Knowing her as I did, there is no way she would have been able to listen to the very heartbeat of a person and not be moved to tears. Undoubtedly she wept with everyone who dared to be open and vulnerable with her. She wept with those who risked her reaction and responses. And undoubtedly she wept with any who bared the private joys and pains of their souls with her. Surely at times tears of joy cascaded down her cheeks, for she often cried when she laughed . . . but cry she did!

David writes in the 56th Psalm:

You have seen me tossing and turning through the night. You have collected all my tears and preserved them in your bottle! You have recorded every one in your book.

Psalm 56:8, TLB

I could see her, in my imagination's eye, using those tissues to weep with troubled people and gently wipe away not only her tears but theirs as well—or, soaking up a tissue or two with her tears of happy laughter from her lovely face.

It's a heart-tugging experience to read David's words about God collecting and recording our tears, so much so that I wish now I'd kept that mound of wadded-up, very precious tissues. But, I didn't. The memory will have to serve as a sweet and soul-stirring reminder—not only of my mother's mission but of mine, as well, that . . .

> God calls us all
> to love and to laugh,
> to comfort and to cry,
> to care and to give, and
> to walk and to wait
> with others.

I spent hours that day (other than soaking up my own tissues) folding, separating and packing away her clothes. Some dresses I'd made for her—or had been shopping with her when she made the purchase—but each dress or skirt, every jacket or blouse released the fragrance of her White Shoulders; and that, in turn, triggered vivid memories of how she looked in her clothes and how I couldn't believe she'd never need these things again.

Between skipping lunch, which I'll bet was Dad's Irish stew, emptying out her closet and packing the contents of her bedroom dresser drawers, I'd been completely unaware of the passing of time. Breaking my concentration for a moment, I found myself turning on the lamp and the closet light; and looking at my watch, I realized I'd missed dinner as well!

Finally, all was sorted and packed. This seemingly everlasting task was finished, and I sank, bone weary, down into the couch. I hadn't been sitting there very long when I became aware of something ragging on the edges of my mind, and it grew more annoying with each passing moment. Frustration and anger were breaking through my tiredness and adding to the deep sadness I'd felt all day. In no time at all, I felt myself becoming quite hostile. I couldn't imagine what was making my emotions boil and why I was

20

feeling such storm clouds of anger. I know now it was the sight of those three cardboard boxes that did it!

All day I'd been preoccupied with intellectually and emotionally thawing out the icicle memories of mother, grieving, crying, laughing at my poor seamstress ability on one dress I'd made, missing her, and packing away her things. It wasn't until the end of that emotionally trying and draining day that I apprised the traces of what was left of her . . . *three ordinary cardboard boxes?* That's it?

It was outrageous! A woman like Marion Miller . . . one woman in several million! A real, no phoney baloney woman. True helpmate and pastor's wife for thirty-eight years. An extraordinary mother. An exciting, devoted grandmother. A brilliant mind. A compassionate heart. A woman well-acquainted with both sorrow and joy. An earthy, yet godly woman. And, yes, my dearest, most trusted friend and major cheerleader in my balcony . . . gone . . . and all that's left of her fitted neatly into three simple cardboard boxes. My heart and mind screamed in unison,

Dear God, what have you allowed to happen here? Are you kidding me? Don't you want to rethink this? Could this really be your plan for her, for us? Does the sum of her entire life add up to these insignificant boxes before me? Is this all we have to remember of her? Are the contents of these crummy boxes her legacy or the total inheritance she's willed to us, to family, to friends?

Barely respectful, smoldering with hot indignation, I gave God a fiery rundown on the pitiful inventory before me.

Box One: A couple of knit dresses to go to Jean Farthingham who was the same size as Mother and a good friend in their church.

Box Two: A few dresses, lingerie and some costume jewelry to go to my wonderful Aunt Grace, Mother's sister.

Box Three: Who could forget the biggest one, going where? Why, to the Goodwill, of course!

"Lord," I blurted out, "there is something decidedly and dreadfully wrong with all of this! It's so unfair! It looks to

21

me as if her whole life has been reduced to next to nothing. And, once these boxes are gone (awful thought) it will be as if Marion Miller never existed . . . as if she never mattered or counted or anything . . . . I can't believe this!"

Fortunately for me, and as a matter of fact for all of us, God has very broad shoulders. Down through the centuries God's children have shouted out their grievances and more than once have virtually picketed his throne room. He is perfectly capable of taking whatever we dish out. Even when it's the most bitter emotional garbage of our souls.

I suspect that our heavenly Father's response to us is somewhat similar to ours—particularly when we, as parents, have to deal with flare-ups of anger by our children.

Often my darling child, Laurie, her blue eyes blazing with anger, let me know in no uncertain terms that my treatment of her was quite unfair and unacceptable. She felt I was discriminating against her and allowing a monstrous injustice in her life because, as she put it, "I have to go to bed while you let Ricky stay up another half hour just because he's older!"

Oh, boy. As a mother, I had to stand there and let her pound away. I had to see her point and try to understand her angry feelings. I had to know those feelings were real, yet temporary. At the same time I had to carry out what I felt was in her best interest. Somehow, I had to try to see the whole scope of her growing up days rather than a fraction of a part.

God, our heavenly father, lets us pound on his chest occasionally. He has a unique edge on his knowledge that we, as parents, don't have. God created us and he is acutely aware of each and every state of mind and emotion within us. He saw the intent of our hearts yesterday. He sees it right now, and he foresees it in all of our tomorrows. David pointed that out, in the 139th Psalm. While we were still being formed in our mother's womb . . . God planned out all our days for us. So, God has been, and is, intimately conscious of our reactions and responses. He knows and understands all about us—the good, the bad,

22

and the in-between workings of our hearts and minds. God sees the *whole circle* of our emotions, rather than the one small wedge of anger.

While I was spewing out my angry feelings and questions to God about "Mother's things," he did not send a bolt of lightning to shut me up or whack me on my backside and send me off to bed with no supper (although its probably close to what I deserved . . .). He didn't use the event as a springboard for a soul-scalding sermon on the evils of doubting his will, of questioning his actions, or of challenging his authority. He also did not ignore me by pretending he didn't know who I was, making me feel invisible. He didn't treat me as though I had a highly infectious case of leprosy, thereby confirming that I was unclean and untouchable. No. Not at all, none of these punitive actions.

God's gracious spirit allowed me some valuable and uninterrupted time to dump on him. He gave me sufficient time in which to vent the whole black cloud of grief and rage, to release the feelings which were seething inside my heart and mind. God, ever the patient father, waited while I went on and on about the gross unfairness and injustices involving "Mother's things."

At last, after I had exhausted my energy and was feeling emotionally spent, I was pleasantly and more than a little surprised that filtering through the empty, now icicle-less halls of my mind, I could hear a new message. It was God's calm, quiet, moving yet firm words. I could hear,

No, Joyce-Honey, this isn't all she's left you. Your inheritance is not to be found in these boxes. Your mother's legacy is a whole warehouse, packed full of treasures. She's left you many, many gifts; and, if you're finished yelling at me and calmed down enough to listen to me, I'd like to tell you about some of them.

I leaned back into the couch pillows feeling foolish and very small—but still my father's precious child—as his strong arms of love sustained and comforted me. I felt even

23

more foolish, if that was possible, and guilty for not seeing the larger picture regarding the losses and the gains during our time in this process we call life. Especially as God reminded me of one exquisite gift after another. I'd been doing my usual thing, focusing on the part instead of the whole.

Just recently, when I asked my husband, Francis, how he would like to be remembered after he was gone and what he would want to be said about him, he thought for a brief moment and then softly answered, "I'd want people to say I made a difference."

I thought, "Yes, that's precisely what's true for me too." I want to live so close to God's heart that I, as did my mother, will make a difference in the lives of others during this sometimes cruel and terrifying journey.

I then remembered the emotion-fraught day of packing away "Mother's things." The feelings of deep loneliness for her, the aching sadness of holding her clothes and smelling her fragrance. And then the clear message about all the gifts, those precious gifts Mother left me. I realized that Francis' words, although he never met her, were exactly what my mother had actually done with her life. She was no longer here, but we knew she'd made a difference.

What a noble difference Marion Miller made. That "weak, unknown handmaiden" as she called herself, had made a lasting difference, an everlasting difference!

We've all heard the old saying that you can't give a gift away if you don't have it. Inheritances are like that. You can't leave houses and land to someone if you don't first *own* them. In the case of my inheritance, the wonderful gifts Mother gave me were straight out of her vast storehouse of possessions. All those gifts, once hers, now belong to me. They are mine. So, now it isn't a question of the legality of my inheritance—that's been established. Or, even how much I've been given—that's a fortune. But, rather, the question becomes: What shall I do with what I have?

During the last year or two, I've been aware of a compelling urge deep within to give this fortune away. So, in the past year of speaking engagements, I've been doing just that—giving away the gifts left to me by Mother. And now, I want to try, through language on these brief pages, to present those gifts to you.

Oh, dear Lord, what an inheritance we've all been given!

Keep us from selfishly hoarding it in some basement room of our hearts, or carelessly squandering it, watching it disappear into the grey oblivion of nothingness . . . or blindly refusing to invest the immense holdings in the first place and being unwilling to share the profits with others as well.

Help us all, Lord, to unwrap these heavenly gifts . . . these beautiful gifts . . . given first by you to your children, and then handed down from one generation to another to us. Help us to put into practice every bejeweled truth our inheritance teaches. And help us (me especially, Lord) to use our time here on earth wisely, sharing and giving away these prized gifts to others in need.

God, I believe that in seeing your face and shining glory and feeling your presence strongly in these gifts, our lives will be changed . . . magnificently changed.

Our broken relationships will have a chance to mend, even to be made whole. Our relationship with you, dear Father, will grow and flourish. And our ever-present need for your beautiful work of restoration and wholeness in our lives will see the green light of progress.

Dear Lord, we do so want to make a difference here.

Looking at those three pathetic boxes, on that night so long ago, it was quite beyond my capability to envision anything as glorious or profound as my mother's life making an earth-shattering difference. Yet now, oh dear God, what an eternal difference I see she has made.

Help me, Lord, by these fleeting words on these brief pages not to depict Mother as Saint Marion—she was too authentic for that. Just help me to wisely open, explore and give away the inheritance she left behind.

I truly believe that if I am able to write this clearly, lucidly enough, we will all see the endless potential and possibilities of *our* inheritance. And we will make, and keep on making, a *lasting* difference, not only in our own lives but in the lives of others the world around.

Chapter 2

I know now that when I visualized with my spiritual eye the first gift wrapped box of my inheritance, I was less than thrilled, perhaps even a little disappointed. I recognized it immediately. I'd seen this gift often, and, in fact, I'd opened the box and lifted out this particular gift many times. The faded wrapping paper was dog-eared and had a tattered feeling as if it had been recycled way beyond the point of reclamation. Even the ribbon was wilted and its edges frayed from my continuous tying and untying.

Since I was so familiar with the contents of this box, I wondered why I should bother to open it. Why give it yet *another* look? It was not some new exciting gift. After all, I'd had access to it all my life. Emotionally it felt as if I had received a present, unwrapped it, and found an old, threadbare pair of black cloth gloves. It wasn't exactly what I had expected. I'd hoped for a smashing new fur-lined pair done up in glorious gleaming white leather. So what did I want with an old pair of used gloves? Yet, it didn't seem right to set it aside and ask God to show me something else. Curiously, I was compelled to undo the weary looking ribbon and see if maybe I could find something of merit, something I'd overlooked in this well-known gift.

The opened box held, as I'd known it would, the rather common gift of humor. Again, a sense of "why bother?" crossed my mind. I was tempted to put it back in the folds of its tissue paper and forget about it. However, somehow it seemed—in my imagination—that the gift sparkled in a different way. My creative mind took over, and in those moments the gift of humor assumed a mysterious luminous quality . . . silver and shimmering like moon beams playing across the surface of a lake. Was it possible that I'd missed something here? Slowly, it dawned upon me that perhaps God wanted to shed a new light on this ordinary gift! He seemed to be saying to me that I'd overlooked some important discoveries about humor, and right there, before my eyes, the gift sparkled even brighter.

A few years ago, when I was researching Egyptian culture, artifacts and history for the novel *Joseph*, I spent several glorious days wandering around the second floor of the British museum, in London, taking copious notes and scores of mental pictures. The beautiful glass floor display cabinets and cases were fully equipped with excellent lighting, and each article on exhibit had a printed card next to it with an explanation of dates plus significant data. It was most impressive, and the time spent there gave me a crash course on ancient Egyptian culture.

Several days later I left England, flew down to Egypt and continued my research at the Cairo Museum. Once there, however, I went into something akin to deep cultural shock. The Egyptian museum was housed in a massive building. It contained nothing but thousands of artifacts relating to Egypt's history, and there was infinitely more to see and more to absorb. It certainly eclipsed the collection I'd seen on the second floor of the British museum.

In one of the Cairo museum's cavernous rooms, with only a few windows for light, I remember looking down into a glass table case and wondering what in the world I was looking at. In the semi-darkness the objects resembled some abstract collection of small rocks and string or metal tubing. There were no identifying cards in Egyptian, or in English for that matter. I was frustrated. I'd brought along a flashlight and was accompanied by an English speaking guide, but at that moment my guide had gone off somewhere, taking the flashlight with her. I was about to give up on trying to figure out the artifacts before me when my guide re-appeared. Instantly, she cast a beam of light down into the case and proceeded to explain exactly what I was seeing.

It was an amazing experience because whatever it was in the cabinet fairly exploded into life. A moment before I had seen a meaningless pile of rocks and whatever—the next moment, because of the light and the verbal stream of information from my guide, the contents of the case almost came alive and made perfect sense. Rising up out of that dusty glass cabinet came poignant and ancient beauty the likes of which I'd rarely seen. What had been colorless rocks and dull metal things to my eyes were now transformed into classical elegance. The flashlight's beam picked up the exquisite groupings of precious gem stones, which had been fitted into finely-worked gold mountings. Apparently, they were necklaces and bracelets made for and worn about two or three thousand years ago by some privileged princess, perhaps a daughter of the ruling Pharaoh. The regal jewelry glowed with rapturous colors. The goldsmith who had fired, beaten and worked the gold had been a master. His art had endured the aesthetic test of the centuries.

I wondered, as I looked at the gift of humor, if it were possible that I'd become so accustomed to seeing it in a darkened room, without any data cards, that I had thought this extraordinary gift to be just an ordinary pile of rocks and metal when, in reality, it was a gleaming exquisite necklace waiting to be removed from the box and placed around my neck.

Humor, or more accurately, having a *sense* of humor, is really a miraculous thing. Everyone it seems, including me, has talked or written about the immense value of humor. I've endlessly, to the point of possibly boring people, emphasized the vital need for this gift in our daily existence in almost every book I've written. But the truth is that even though it is one of God's most considerate benefactions to mankind, we've become too jaded about its real value. I realized that I, for one, had taken it for granted far too long, and in the process I'd relegated the miracle of the gift of humor into a box labeled "commonplace."

"Open the box, Joyce-Honey," I could hear my mother say. (I loved the way she always called me by a hyphenated name!) "Joyce-Honey, there's much more to learn, and, believe me, in the years out ahead you're going to need your inheritance of humor. Darling daughter, untie the wilted bow, take off the worn wrappings, lift out the gift and examine it under a new light."

Nowhere in my memories do I recall my mother or my father sitting me down and teaching me with chalk and blackboard the lessons on the importance of humor. Yet, from my earliest recollections of childhood, humor was as much a part of our family life as was my mother's creamy, smooth and delicious Farina cereal, sprinkled with brown sugar and raisins and brimming with milk—which she served every cold morning of our lives.

My father was our resident comedian. Before he became a Christian and a preacher, he had been profoundly influenced by Fatty Arbuckle, one of the first Vaudevillian-type comics on the silent silver screen. The love of performing and being a stand-up comedian never left Dad. The pictures that we have of him, taken in Owen Sound, Ontario, Canada, when he was a pastor and I was seven or eight years old, show him clowning around at the dinner table. The home movies filmed at the same time show his gift for miming as he was captured on film doing something with his hands and feet that had to be akin to doing an Irish jig. Heaven forbid! Dancing in those days, in our Christian circle, was thought to be a "most grievous sin" especially for anyone who was *truly* "saved", or worse . . . a pastor. His funny antics—such as playing invisible trombones, making his voice and mouth produce Hawaiian guitar music, or his imaginative pantomimes, the quick grin, and his bubbly spirit in those days—took the boredom out of being a preacher's kid and living in a two-room flat on the third floor. And if being our in-house zany man, singing songs or being a merry dancer didn't work to make us see the brighter side of life, he'd pick up his violin and play a spirited version of *Humoresque*. He went at life with such charm and vigor that he made us all laugh no matter how bleak those times were.

My mother gladly let my father be the *comedian del'arte* and encouraged him to perform under the comedy spotlight. She dearly loved him and had indeed fallen in love with him at Bible college in 1928, according to her diary, because of two things—his Irish blue eyes and his creative talents. But somewhere, early in her life as a woman, pastor's wife and mother, she began to forge out her own definitions of humor and, somewhat like the process of osmosis, I absorbed them.

My siblings and I understood that if Dad was the comedian, mother was his straight "man"; for she knew she had very little talent for performing comedy. She was incapable of telling jokes that made sense or were in any way remotely funny. Worse, she didn't understand most of the humorous anecdotes or stories anyone else told. I grew up loving to watch her responses, in a group of people or privately, when someone told a joke. It was almost impossible to detect that she was anything but totally absorbed in the story or that her wonderful laughter was anything but completely genuine. But I knew that it would only be a matter of hours—sometimes minutes—before she would get us aside and confidentially whisper to my father or me, "Now, what did the man mean when he said, 'The chicken crossed the road to get to the other side'?" We would fall apart laughing. She tried so hard to figure out what was funny, and of course the more we tried to explain the line the more puzzled she'd become. We often found explaining the point or the punch line of a joke to her was infinitely more fun than the joke had been in the first place.

Long after I was grown and not too long before she died, I found myself saving jokes or editing stories just to tell her and hoping she would "get" them and think them (and me) funny. I clearly remember reading a joke in *Readers Digest* about two stuffy British gentlemen in their English men's club. Because mother was a fan of English literature and understood the typical reserved nature of the English people, I thought I'd found the perfect joke. I just knew she'd catch the punch line and fall over in cognizant laughter.

While with her one day I remembered the story and launched in. "Mother, there were these two frightfully proper English gentlemen sitting in big wingback chairs at their private men's club. They were both reading. Then, without putting their papers down, one gentleman said to the other,

Buried my wife yesterday.
Is that so?
Yes. Had to. She was dead, you know.

I thought it was a classic comment on reserved English humor (although as I read it now, on these pages, it doesn't seem like too much of a knee slapper). I waited for my mother's bubbling laughter at my perfect joke. It never came. Instead, her eyes filled up with tears and she said, with great compassion, "Oh, that poor man. How sad." For two days I had to go back over the whole thing and tell her again and again that is was *just* a story. A joke. That was the easy part. The harder part was trying to convince her that the man's wife didn't really die. I never tried to tell her a joke after that.

In one of her notebooks, I found her idea of a joke, a written example of what she thought humorous. She'd written, and I'm sure repeated to her Bible study class,

The Lord gave us two ends to use. One to sit with and one to think with. Our success depends on which end we choose.

Heads we win, tails we lose.

But, even when she did recite these few lines, or any other humorous work, she'd have to be sure she read it word for word so she'd get it straight; and, of course, it lost considerably in the translation. Her reading of a funny story or joke brought new meaning to the phrase "You had to be there."

My precious mother, as I've said in countless talks and in several books, was not a Phyllis Diller or Roseanne Barr comedienne, nor was she a humorous writer like Erma Bombeck. But she did possess an enormous capacity for gentling out and toning down some of the harshness of life by possessing a marvelous and ready *sense* of humor.

Having a sense of humor has little to do with our ability to understand, write or deliver humorous, bantering jokes or amusing stories. I believe, in retrospect, that my mother felt a twinge of relief when she figured out the vast difference between *being* humorous and *having* a sense of humor. When she no longer had to *be* funny, to understand jokes and to come back with one liners, she must have recognized that having a *sense* of humor about one's whole life was a gift and that one should, as Paul wrote to Timothy, "stir up the gift of God which is in you." Actually, on her twenty-second birthday her prayer in her diary reads, "Stir me Lord, Stir me Lord, Stir me Lord." I wonder if she knew how many areas and ways God could and did "stir up" her gifts?

Our whole society tries to be humorous. A plethora of humor crops up jungle wild around us. We find it in our families, friendships, T.V. screens, movies, all forms of entertainment, business, job, church, government, politics . . . everywhere. But much of the humor around us lies in our *being* constantly funny, and this is *not* the criteria for having a *sense* of humor.

A person with a healthy *sense* of humor is one who views life's realities in such a way that people and events are seen through a lens which says: I will try, to the best of my ability not to act and feel as if everything which happens to me is life threatening or terribly serious. I will also endeavor to find the "light side" in difficult times for myself and others, to give at least temporary relief from the maddening stresses and grievous woundings of life. But I will be cautious with this gift lest I abuse anyone or myself—in the name of humor.

In one way humor can be compared to the rapidly expanding field of laser beam technology. We know that if a laser ray is fashioned into a weapon, a knowledgeable firearms expert can direct its power at a target, thus maiming or killing. However, if that same laser is put into a medical instrument, a surgeon can use it to "zap" cataracts from a patient's eyes without damaging the surrounding tissues. Laser beam technology is a dramatic example of the potential utilization of science for negative or positive purposes.

Anything around us, or within us, can be used or abused. I am still dealing with the recognition that from time to time I've fallen into some pretty obvious traps about humor. One of those pitfalls was smugly feeling that there was not a whole lot to be learned about humor. I've discovered that there is a vast hole in my education about the difference between *being* funny and *having* a sense of humor. And since humor, like the laser beam, is a very complex subject, I've discovered that both humor and laser beams have the propensity to be healing or lethal. One can die of an overdose of humor or laser treatment, especially when either one is mishandled or abused.

The fact that humor (like a cheerful heart) is good medicine does not automatically mean that just any kind of humor is good or healing in every situation. Humor's deadly side—and this is worthy of much self-examination—can turn ugly and destructive quickly. Before we know it, we have used it to cripple or destroy another's selfhood.

It's possible that opening up the gift of humor forced me to come face-to-face with some hard to handle realities. I burned with a feeling of shame when I realized that somewhere along the way I'd not only lost my *sense* of humor, but I'd abused the gift of humor and unwittingly (maybe even unconsciously) wounded another's psyche on some occasions.

In my personal life, I can recall unconsciously disguising
ridicule,
needling,
teasing,
harassing,
pestering,
attacking,
in a bizarre costume I slipped into calling "humor." I also
remember other specific incidents which were disguised as
humor and reflect that I said some thoughtlessly cruel
things to my father, brother, family and some friends. Sadly
enough, all I think I accomplished by my "humorous comments" was to injure someone's fragile personhood, to shat-
ter one's peace of mind, or to add to one's load of emotional
insecurities and guilt.

I believe that not only on the home front but on the
national level a large portion of the humor we use or hear
being used is no longer doing "good like a medicine" as in
Proverbs 17:22.

Humor is a vital, visceral and integral part of life. We
experience humor, we use humor, in multiplied manifesta-
tions and occurrences. We hear humor from others, and we
need humor's balm to heal us emotionally, physically and
spiritually. Sadly, the humor of our day commits some
pretty negative crimes. For instance, much of our humor
does not

warm our hearts with laughter, or
soften the blows of criticism, or
build bridges across our differences, or
open our minds with understanding, or
remove the stinging needles of rejection, or
help us to forget, for a moment, about the pain, or
break down the walls of prejudice, or
plant seeds of hope to blossom later.

No, it doesn't. An incredible amount of our humor is
definitely not the healing medicine God intended it to be.

Privately and publicly, by what we call humor, we make light of pain, nationality, life, work, etc. We emotionally ridicule others by the bent of our own bias and the shadowside of our own predispositions. There are jokes about everybody and every life circumstance. There are jokes about the emotionally and mentally handicapped and the physically disabled. There are Polish jokes, Black jokes, doctor and lawyer jokes, Jewish jokes, Catholic and Pope jokes, Protestant and preacher jokes, family and mother-in-law jokes, government, politicians and foreign country jokes, student and educator's jokes, sick and deranged jokes, and many more too numerous to mention here.

It seems that at the core of so much of our present-day humor is a mushrooming trend toward sarcasm in the form of "put downs." Just last night on TV a new sit-com series aired, and almost every funny punch line used sarcasm as the method to get the laugh. On another show, a stand-up comedian's whole routine was a collection of put downs. He started with his parents, went on to his teachers and employers, and ended with one ugly line after another about women. A third program featured a talk-show host whose opening comments were a string of sarcastic stories aimed at a score of people. There were put downs at the expense of everyone—from politicians to bald headed men—and it was done in the name of being funny to make others laugh.

It's no secret that when we camouflage sarcasm as wit, our motive, conscious or not, is to inflict pain on others through malevolent "humor." It's as if we think present day humor isn't funny unless it's a very personal insult to someone else. It's almost as if we get a rush of perverse joy when someone makes light of another human being, taking aim at their greatest point of vulnerability.

Obviously, I'm aware of the dangers of throwing *all* humor into one generalized pot; however, I feel our use of humor as a weapon instead of a healer is almost at pandemic levels. Is it not easy to see that when humor is at its cruelest level, it's the story teller who sees the humor or who thinks the ridiculing is funny? The person on the receiving end rarely, if ever, laughs. If you, per chance, are the victim of the sarcasm, and you voice your objections to being "humorously attacked," you'll probably open yourself up to a fresh round of verbal pounding. You'll hear "Whatsa matter, can't you take a joke? Where's your sense of humor?" or, "Hey, I was *just* kidding. Why are you so sensitive?"

Now, it's true there are many times in our lives when our sense of humor and our level of maturity enables us to laugh at ourselves and to "take a joke." But we shouldn't be expected to take another's battering which hits below the belt and leaves us broken and bleeding. When something is said, in the name of humor, and it annihilates a human being, it ceases to be humor and becomes deadly taunting. I doubt that anybody I've ever known, or will know, in this lifetime enjoys or deserves that kind of inner devastation.

In one of my discussions about humor with my husband, Francis, he was very disturbed about the abuse of humor, and made this statement, "Humor too often is viewed as something to be done without conscience." To me, that's the very heart of this issue. Perhaps that's why sarcastic humor, practiced from our junior high days onward, is of such a concern to those of us who care about the wellbeing of others. Whether we like it or not, we do have a responsibility to ourselves and to others to weigh our words, passing them through the inner sanctuary of our conscience so that they will nourish rather than wound.

My daughter, Laurie, has a sixty percent hearing loss in one ear, and a forty percent loss in the other. Just recently I asked her if anyone made offensive comments about it or made fun of her hearing problem. I could tell my questions struck a raw cord deep in her heart because of the darkening in her blue eyes and an almost imperceptible pulling back of her shoulders, but I pressed, "Laurie-Honey, what percentage of people in your social and working circles make 'humorous remarks' about your deafness?"

"About ninety-five percent," she answered softly.

"That high?"

"Yes."

"Tell me, what's it like?"

Slowly, thoughtfully, Laurie answered, "Well, Mom, when I have missed what someone's said, I know I've got to ask them to repeat themselves. I feel very vulnerable, but I explain, 'Excuse me, I'm sorry, I didn't hear you.' Or, I say, 'I beg your pardon, but I have a hearing loss.'

"What hurts me most, Mom, is that ninety-five percent respond to me about my hearing loss in one of two ways. Either they cup their hand behind one ear pretending they are old and deaf, and they lean towards me shouting, 'Eh? What's that you said? Huh? Huh?' Or, they tell me to turn up my hearing aid."

"And that hurts, doesn't it?"

"Well," Laurie nodded her head yes, "the other night one of the guys at work started in again about my not being able to hear, and I finally just whirled around and said *'Mark, it's not funny!'* I was furious with him."

We have much to learn about the destructive side of humor. If we are going to tease or ridicule anyone about anything, we need to find out how they feel about being teased. If their point of suffering is a devastating loss, a physical disfigurement, mental or emotional impairment, or a myriad of other painful problems, then our "humorous" teasing exposé or revelation is, as Laurie said, "Not funny."

Just this morning I read, "A man who is caught lying to his neighbor and says 'I was just fooling' is like a madman throwing around firebrands, arrows and death" (Proverbs 26:18,19, TLB).

Perhaps it's a blessing that my mother was not able to be a "performer" with her humor. She was a splendid example for me and quietly taught that, as a Christian woman, abusing others with humor or saying things in a humorous vein *without conscience* should have no part in my life. I am sobered and stunned by the mandate I hear in my heart when I read, "Some people like to make cutting remarks, but the words of the wise soothe and heal" (Proverbs 12:18, TLB). Despite tradition, all is *not* "fair in love and war" and the pursuit of humor.

Some of my biographical sheets and promotional information describe me as "using warm humor and gentle conviction." I truly hope so! But I must be very careful about using humor the wrong way even when it's done unintentionally. Just as strongly as my mother's teachings were about having no part in abusing someone in the name of humor, she was equally as firm and committed to teaching me about praying for wise words which would "soothe and heal" and about continually renewing my efforts at developing my sense of humor.

Perhaps it was a special day or maybe a rather ordinary one, I don't know, but one day I suspect my mother *chose* her attitudes about the subject of humor. And more than anything else she taught she silently typed into my mind's computer the message that "having a sense of humor" about events and people is largely a matter of *attitude choice.* More precisely, she taught me that I did have the ability to deliberately *choose* and *exercise* this attitude. When you think about it, there is precious little else in life that we hold as strong a control over as our choice of attitude and thus, of personal uses of humor.

In living out the last five traumatic years of my life which involved separation, divorce, and my marriage to Francis, it would have been easy for me to erase the mental sequence of my mother's early programming. The idea of choosing not to "take myself too seriously" when unthinkable losses cheated my joys, or trying to view life through a "humorous screen" when I was plunged in despair, was as seemingly impossible for me to do as it was against my natural inclinations.

During those awful days, I received a number of hateful, scorn tinged letters from former friends and associates. Days merged into years with animate silences. I felt rejec-

38

tion on every level of my life. However, one of the greatest hurts of all was that of being in public around people I knew, and watching them as they deliberately looked through and past me. I always felt as if I were playing the lead in a low budget movie called *The Invisible Woman.*

Nowhere was the rejection or its pain stronger or more obvious than when it was transmitted through "Christians." Particularly painful were our experiences at church. It's only fair to say that two or three pastors and their wives ("Please God," as our friend Pastor John Hagee would say, "Kiss them on their foreheads with your blessing.") ministered to us in eloquent and significant ways. But, on the whole, attending church was so damaging that we lost heart and quit going. Basically we dropped out of celebrating Sunday altogether. Church and Sunday School attendance were too shattering, and being wounded by rejection to the point of invisibility was too injurious to our spiritual and emotional health. Staying home was bearable though not our preferred choice. Frankly, I felt it would probably never be possible for us to regain a semblance of balance in our religious and social lives or to ever find the "joy of our salvation" again. Fortunately, I was wrong. Our loving heavenly father's "mercy endureth forever" and somehow he sees to it that his children never loose the honeyed inlay of his sweet presence.

At this point, I wish the print on this paper would turn fluorescent pink or green. I wish these words could assume life and befriend you. Now, looking back on those days which were almost more than flesh and blood could endure, I can see clearly that I survived by the direct intervention of God. It was as if God stole up behind me, on my blind side, and intimately intoned, "Joyce, my beloved child, it was I who gave your mother the insights she taught you about choosing to have a sense of humor. Watch and wait for the ways I will restore your life. I am your resurrection and your life in life, now and forever. Remember, it is

I who stands between you and those who would harm you."
God's been intervening with his children since the beginning of time. Read his heart warming words to Jeremiah.

For I know the plans I have for you, says the Lord . . . to give you a future and a hope.

Jer. 29:11

Francis and I might still be paralyzed by fear except for something on which we hadn't counted: God's intervention through an old uninhibited, straight-shooting woman named Flora. But before I tell you about her let me set the stage with some background material.

Quite a war raged within me. The Joyce who was bruised and hurting refused to go to church. She did not want to be wounded again by "God's people" and die over and again on some pew bench. But the other Joyce struggled with her deep longing for God. She was lonely for the pleasure of participating with others in a church service. She was lonely for the presence of the Holy Spirit during the prayer time. She missed singing the hymns with other believers. She longed to hear the organ music. She hungered for the communion service. She was starving for a sermon which would feed and minister to her spiritual needs and overwhelming sense of brokenness. In fact, she was so lonely for God and to be in his house that thoughts of placing money in the offering plate were enticing.

Finally, one Saturday night, when I could stand it no longer, I verbally described my troubled feelings and poured out my loneliness for God to Francis. True to form, within seconds he came up with a plan.

"Let's get up early tomorrow morning, drive out into the country, and find a small church in some little Texas town."

I was thrilled with his idea and instantly did my usual thing. I decided what I'd wear.

"We'll wait a few minutes until after the service has begun and then we'll go in," he suggested. "Let's sit by the back door and then leave during the pastor's closing prayer. Okay?" "But, what," I questioned, "if someone thinks they recognize me, asks me my name and the rejection starts in all over again?"

"All right, here's what we'll do," he continued. "If we are asked who we are, I'll just speak up and say, 'We're Francis and Joyce.' Period. No last names, just 'Francis and Joyce.' And we'll let them worry about which is Francis and which is Joyce."

It was an exceptional plan. It also worked far more smoothly than we thought or dreamed.

The next morning a beautiful Texas Sunday dawned, and after driving through a few towns we turned off the highway and headed for a place whose city limit sign read, "Population 675." It was perfect. Driving past a couple of pillar-impressive churches on Main Street, we made a turn onto a side road and found just the place we wanted.

Francis parked the car, and we got out and made our way towards the front door of the little country church. I prayed, the nearer we got to the entrance, that there would be two inconspicuous seats on the back row.

The service was, as we'd hoped, already in progress and —wonder of wonders—there were two vacant seats on the last row right where they were supposed to be!

However, no sooner than we had gratefully slid into the pew, we realized the pastor, in the middle of greetings and announcements, had stopped mid-sentence. Pointing to us, he called out in his booming *"well-hello-there"* voice, "I see we have a lot of visitors here this morning, and two more just came in!" He gestured toward us, inviting us to volunteer our names. Starting to panic, I looked at Francis. But he was the picture of cool composure just sitting there smiling.

Quickly, the pastor figured that (for whatever reason) the strangely quiet couple on the back row was not going to succumb to his friendly charm and give away their vital statistics, so of course he went directly to Plan B.

Craning his neck to get a better look, the pastor took mental inventory of who was sitting next to us and was delighted when he recognized the older lady to my left. "Flora," the pastor boisterously called out, "Uh, Flora, introduce us to your friends!"

Now about Flora, I have to tell you that she was in one of the most enviable times of life. It's that wonderful place somewhere between the eightieth year and the year of not giving a rat's toenail what anybody else thinks of you. Flora had probably lived her whole life—like most of us—trying to please others, hoping for their approval, and deathly afraid of what people would say or think about her. But somewhere, probably lately, it was as if Flora had stepped across an invisible threshold and put a respectable end to worrying about what *anybody* thought about *anything*. She emitted the unmistakable fragrance which announced that she simply could not be intimidated by anything or anyone. She was one of those free spirits who could say and do precisely what she pleased.

This time in life seems to give people like Flora a secret coded message. It's as if they've seen and heard all there is to see and hear, and that leads them to the philosophy that if others don't want raw naked honesty then, by George, they better not ask for it. Flora didn't care about pulling any punches, protecting her saintly image, or putting her best antique foot forward. She'd reached the time in her life when she unreservedly told it like it was.

I think somewhere deep inside of me Flora lives and is raring to get out. A jubilant fantasy of mine is to be Flora's age and no longer worry about what others think or say about me. I'm looking forward to the day when, if I want to go to church plain-faced—without even a slash of lipstick across my mouth, all dressed up in a purple suit with a red hat and a broken strap on my green shoes—I shall do just that. What a thought!

Ahhhh . . . such a great age. But, I digress. Back to Flora.

This quaint and darling elderly lady heard her pastor

ask her to introduce the congregation to her friends seated beside her. So, after taking a head to toe look at me and leaning forward to see Francis, she—who had absolutely nothing to lose by being candid—called out forthrightly to the pastor, "They're not *my* friends!"

Flora had, in only four words, dramatically and succinctly summed up most of my recent personal and public relationships. I almost fell off the pew laughing. It was the story of my life. We had pathetically few friends, but here was a woman who inadvertently documented it in public.

Francis and I laughed about it all the way home. Weeks later we'd just look at each other and start chuckling. If the word "friends" was mentioned or was used on television, we'd just break up, remembering darling Flora. Actually we're still laughing.

How incredible of God to intervene with humor when we were at the apex of our pain, when our losses of many long-time friends and associates were so acutely present and pressing on our minds. And how like God to do it unexpectedly through a total stranger, in such a delightful way that it eased our response into laughter. Healing laughter. It was the kind of laughter that made our hearts cheerful and merry . . . doing good to our spirits like a medicine and bringing a measure of wellness to our stricken souls.

I've had my share of embarrassing incidents—like the time my slip fell off at the taping of a Johnny Cash TV special, or when I fell flat on my face on the platform steps in front of Dr. Billy Graham and 750 pastors and their wives. But most of those events were harmless and only mildly embarrassing. They did not involve an attack on my personhood. They simply provided me and others with a humorous moment, leaving me feeling slightly foolish with my dignity and pride a little tarnished.

But, during the last four years, I doubt I've had a more grievous struggle in my life than the one over the abrupt absence of friends. The loss of those dear ones decimated my self-esteem and I felt utterly worthless. So, to see God providing us with a short but wonderful time of laughter and reflections with a "Flora break" was indeed, a refreshing surprise and miraculous healing! Especially when both Francis and I realized we were laughing over something which was incredibly painful to us. It was on that Sunday that God helped us to learn the value of having a sense of humor in the *midst* of our pain.

We all enjoy laughing *at* a funny story—and the experience gives us a measure of relief. It's also true, as James Thurber said, that humor is "emotional chaos remembered in tranquility." We can, in time, look back over our shoulder and see the humor of the chaos, and we can laugh *at* the incident and again feel relief from stress and life pressures. But there is a vast difference between hindsight laughter and in choosing to view all of life *with* a sense of humor. The difficult maneuver is finding the funny side of life *during* the troubling and uncertain times. (It seems to me that Mrs. Noah must have had a well-developed *sense* of humor. How else could she have survived living with Mr. Noah, their sons and daughters-in-law for over a month in a floating zoo?)

I believe we *can* consciously develop and nurture a sense of humor within us which will help us to expand our horizons. It can show us ways to see more, to understand at a deeper level, to appreciate others more keenly, and to better experience our world and daily living. If we choose this attitude we will, as my friend Barb Johnson, founder of Spatula Ministries, continually reminds me, "find the joy in adversity." The other line she keeps casting my way is: "Laughter is that great exercise of jogging on the inside." (Barb, you are great medicine for my heart!)

David wrote in Psalm 126, "How we laughed and sang for joy. . . . Those who sow tears shall reap joy. Yes, they go out weeping, carrying seed for sowing, and return singing, carrying their sheaves."

Jesus' words are healing to us, in our brokenness. He says, "What happiness there is for you who weep, for the time will come when you shall laugh with joy!" Oh for a thousand tongues to tell the joys he has showered upon Francis and me.

The time will come to you, dear hurting person, when you can open and enjoy the gift of having a sense of humor —no matter how difficult your life is, or how long the battle rages, or how grievously you are wounded. God will intervene, perhaps even with a "Flora", and you will laugh with the pure unpremeditated laughter of a child; and your laughter will give you just enough hope and just enough joy to carry on and to keep you running your good race. Then, it is entirely possible that you will catch the vision of *choosing* to view life's journey through the lenses of humor. I am certain that if you make this deliberate choice, it will revolutionize the quality of goodness in your life. It will affect your ability to get back on your feet again, and it will take the sting out of everyday survival.

Chapter 3

From the moment it took shape before my eyes the next box of my inheritance was an aesthetic marvel. It was not wrapped in paper and ribbon, as the gift of humor had been, but was all covered over in an exquisitely embroidered fabric. The colors and designs were unmistakably the work of a Hungarian artist. Vivid red hearts were entwined with flowers, white lilies of the valley, accentuated by their dark green leaves and stems—and brilliant electric blue cornflowers were set like gems here and there among the shimmering-with-life yellow daisies. All were fashioned of lustrous satin yarns, and they seemed to burst out into blossoms from their rich black velvet background.

The package had such an intensely Hungarian personality that I could almost hear it ecstatically shouting, "Open me up! I'm your mother's most original gift! And frankly, even if I do say this myself, while I may get you into trouble from time to time . . . I wear well before God and people . . . I'm the gift of honesty!"

Oh, yes, I should have known that somewhere among the many gifts my mother left me she'd see to it that at least one was extremely Hungarian. It was quite appropriate that it be the gift of honesty, and it was no wonder the box was all wrapped up in Hungarian embroidery. I realized for the first time that I'd never been able to separate my mother's outspoken honesty from her colorful Hungarian temperament and Old World traditions. When I thought back about my "roots," I realized that of all the strong influences during my upbringing, my Hungarian heritage was the richest and the most pronounced. Outspoken honesty and an intense longing for truth were the touchstones of my mother's character, and nowhere was it more brilliantly displayed than in her Hungarianness.

Most certainly, I'm not saying that honesty is the driving force of all Hungarians. I'm also not saying that all Hungarians are locked into certain ethnic characteristics nor even that they all have the same predictable responses to life.

In fact, just because my Hungarian grandmother Uzon made *the* most fragrant and delicious Chicken Paprikas in the world, breaded pork chops which were a feast memorable enough to stay in a gourmet's mind forever, and Dios Kifle (nut-filled pastry crescents) and Retes (strudel, particularly the ground poppy seed and raisin type) sweet ambrosial desserts I'd gladly kill to eat . . . still, that does not mean that all Hungarians are gifted cooks and culinary geniuses.

However, as I think about it, people of various national origins *do* have some highly distinguishing ethnic temperaments, characteristics and cultural mores which are peculiar to them and which highly color and influence their personalities and responses. As a long time people-watcher, I've observed that there are many rich flavorings to be found and savored (like the liberal dose of paprika in Hungarian goulash) when people are bonded together by cultural origin or, sometimes, even by their temporary circumstances.

Generalizations about nationalities are an injustice to any human being. For instance, it is inaccurate and insensitive to say *all* Canadians or Africans are such and such, or *all* Jews, Protestants, Buddhists, Catholics, Muslims, etc. believe and practice such and such, because in reality, that's just not true.

So, when I describe the gift of honesty as being Hungarian, I'm not limiting it to only the Magyars of Hungary, as if other nationalities are dishonest and that Hungarians have cornered the market on honesty. Rather I am saying that, at least in my mother's case, her honesty and her Hungarian lineage and heritage were inseparable. They went together like a piece of Grandma Uzon's fragrantly delicious apple or

47

walnut strudel, served on a Herend china plate with a cup of hot coffee, and . . . "Heavy on the cream and sugar, please."

I have described my mother and written many stories about her over the years. In one book, I called her a "most articulate Hungarian woman." Yet, unless you were a member of my dad's congregation or in her Bible study or counseling classes, or you'd read about her in my books, my mother lived and died without attracting national or worldwide attention.

This unique woman who became my mother, was born to Peter and Veronica Uzon in the tiny village of Ada about thirty kilometers east of Budapest, Hungary in the early nineteen hundreds.

Both my mother Marion and her younger brother, Peter, who is now in his eightieth year, were purebred Hungarians, not just by birth but by the evidence of their specific characteristics. They were Hungarian from their heads to their toes, so much so that I suspect their most obvious Hungarian attribute—being able to verbalize their thoughts with picturesque, relevant and logical forthrightness—probably got them into more trouble than they cared to admit. Actually, outspoken honesty may have been more profitable for my Uncle Pete as he grew up to be a successful and highly articulate attorney. But for my mother, a woman and a pastor's wife, speaking up (honestly or not) just wasn't "the thing to do." In fact, during the nineteen twenties and thirties major sermons were preached in churches across the land, using Paul's text to Timothy about women keeping silent in the house of God. The Victorian adage, "Children should be seen and not heard," went for women as well in those times. It went doubly for a preacher's wife, because she was expected to set an example.

While I was growing up I heard a number of stories from people who were critical of my mother's openness and the unfettered way she usually spoke her mind. People were most annoyed when she spoke up at church business meetings, because it was such a no-no in those days. She said what she believed was truth. The times her blunt honesty got her into trouble seemed to have taught her some pretty useful though painful lessons.

"God, take care of our mouths and what comes out of them," was the prayer my mother prayed for me as I began singing and speaking at "mother and daughter" banquets years ago.

It amused me to hear her pray that way because I had the sneaky feeling she'd paid a price to learn the wisdom of God concerning the guarding our mouths. She had given many a Bible study on that beautiful passage in James describing the characteristic of wisdom, and somehow she had put wisdom and honesty together. She was as serious about being honest as she was about being wise, and she took James 3:17 to heart: "But the wisdom that comes from heaven is first of all pure and full of quiet gentleness. Then it is peace-loving and courteous. It allows discussion and is willing to yield to others; it is full of mercy and good deeds" (James 3:17, TLB).

Like any loving mother, she wanted me to be extremely wise. She engraved on my heart James' admonition that one allow discussion and yield to others. Yet, it was quite apparent that of her three children I was the one who inherited the double edged-sword of her bold, straight-from-the-shoulder verbal patterns. So, when she prayed for "our mouths" it was, to be sure, not a request for my brother Cliff (the one who loves to be *behind* the curtains rather than out on center stage); nor was it for my sister Marilyn Celeste (the one who speaks in such soft and gentle tones that I'm sure unseen angels cluster around her wishing they had her mouth). No, Mother didn't mean them. She meant her own mouth and mine . . . and, in my case, she wanted to rally all the spiritual help she could gather.

Besides praying for "our mouths," my mother's wisdom came to the fore in teaching her children about the strengths and weaknesses of the gift of honesty. She took care to show us the joyful freedom that honesty accords, and she wanted us to cherish and appreciate our outspoken Hungarian characteristics and trademarks.

Mother, like multitudes of people who came to America and passed through Ellis Island in New York, experienced humiliation as the object of uncalled for scorn and ridicule. Especially demeaning to the proud Hungarians was the labeling of them as "Hunkys." Unfortunately, prejudice towards people whose birth origins differ from our own still exists today. At my mother's funeral, one of my father's Irish relatives demonstrated this interesting phenomenon quite audaciously when she allowed that "Marion was a pretty good wife and mother, even though she was a foreigner and a Hunky."

By whatever means, my mother dearly wanted to instill in me a pride and joy in Hungarian heritage. It worked. I do treasure my Hungarian roots. She also desired that I would understand the flip side of the gift of speaking honestly. She believed it was my responsibility to avoid, at all cost, the problem side of honesty . . . Hungarian or not. From remembered talks with her, I know Mother felt that often our most powerful character trait or our greatest talent can simultaneously be our greatest liability and our weakest fallibility. No where did she believe this to be more true than when we were being "honest," "frank" or "candid." If speaking honestly was our strongest attribute, then our words—even honest ones— also could be our greatest Achilles' heel, our most vulnerable spot.

When it turned out that I appeared to have a gift for public speaking, she praised my abilities in this endeavor. But, she also cautioned that speaking, because it *did* come so naturally for me, could turn out to be one of my biggest headaches. She got that right.

As it turned out, even now there are some speaking engagements when I say something stupid, or forget to say something important, and I wonder if I've learned anything at all this century?

My inheritance gift of honesty brought to mind several important concepts from my mother. First, there was her

50

dedicated and unswerving honesty to God. Secondly, there was her honesty about herself. When she was twenty-one years old she attended Central Bible Institute in Springfield, Missouri, and it was there that she began the diary I have before me now. How that diary made it down through the years of my parents moving from one pastorate to another to land on Mother's bookshelves the year of her death is no small wonder to me! Her handwriting is delicately beautiful, and even if the ink is somewhat faded, the poetic prose and style of her writing comes alive as if it were written just yesterday.

She begins writing on January 21, 1928—

Dear Diary,

Somehow I feel as though I would like to write to you each eve, and in that way have a little talk with you about the "Day" and its events. Today was a day just as other days, busy.

I got up at 6:00 am and went down to wait tables in the college dining room; was glad it was my last duty on Saturday morning for another week. After I fixed my tables and cleaned my room, I went to town and bought this little notebook, a pair of pillow slips to embroider, stockings, etc. Practiced piano a little while, pressed my dress, got ready and went down to supper just as usual. I was somewhat tired, but "He giveth strength to His own." Now, praise God, I feel fine. Oh, dear Diary, isn't He a wonderful Savior to me? Just think, He loves me. Oh, to be true to Him and His love always. I don't want to hurt His heart, I want to please Him and do all I can to show Him my love for Him. Yes, He loves me. Oh, it makes my heart beat faster, it makes me happy. Even if nobody else loves me—I know of One, yes One, who loves me even better than I Him.

I have just read a few pages in the book, The Mark of the Beast [a best selling book in the 1920s on the second coming of Christ]. Truly I feel He's coming back soon and oh, I want to be found ready. I want to be found in His love, in His service, in Africa.

Dear Lord, please send me to Africa as a missionary soon. Oh, Lord, prepare me and make me fit for the land to which You have called me. My heart is already there, I long to be there, I want to be there, my place is there.

Well, dear Diary, I could write and still write and yet I couldn't begin to tell you of God's love to me. But from day to day I will write here what He has done and will do for me.

The lights blinked in the dorm, that means 10:00 pm and lights out. They're out now — and Dot's flashlight is giving me dandy service. Good night, dear Diary. I hope Jesus is in my dreams. Will write to you again tomorrow.

As you can tell, Marion Uzon, even at such a young age, was highly committed to God. Off the pages of her diary rises the fragrance of her love, her trust and her absolute gut-level honesty with her maker. He was the God who loved her, who knew all about her and who could be trusted with the changes and even the heartbreaks of life. Interwoven all through the pages is the secondary theme—her honesty, not only with God but with herself.

On the famous twenty-third Psalm of David, my mother's diary reveals that she was willing to trust God not only with the "great days but the days of testing and trials as well." She wrote,

The text this morning given by Brother Moody in chapel, was a wonderful help to me. Psalm 23:4, "Yea, though I walk through the valley . . . ." It's true yet strange, that fiery tests bring you, and bind you closer to the Lord.

She seemed at ease letting it all hang out before God in her diary, and I doubt she held very much back or even edited it—as most of us would do. She included the real spiritual desires of her heart, her dreams of going to Africa as a missionary and her growing romantic feelings for a handsome student. Very early, she begins to mention "Mr. M" or "Mr. C," as she calls him in her diary, and she hints that she could be very interested in him. However, she also describes the irony that while they are attracted to each other, she has found out that they both have been called to

52

be missionaries on separate foreign fields. She is dedicated to going straight to Africa; and it seems Mr. C is equally dedicated to being a missionary, but he's on his merry way to China.

Her diary drops in tiny samples of her sense of humor— self-effacing and yet warm, but giving me a truly, colorful living portrait of the young woman called "Miss Uzon," such as the entry which reads,

> *Margaret told me about the conversation at her table—about "somebody" who plays the piano from 2:00 to 2:40 pm in the chapel each day and who is playing one piece to death. It was me! And I tell you, diary, I won't play that piece again for a long time, even though the young man who mentioned it told Margaret that he was sorry he'd said anything about it when he found out it was "Miss Uzon."*

Or, an excerpt from another page which says,

> *Dear Diary,*
>
> *Yesterday, I was so busy getting my lessons for the Doctrine test that I had no time to spend with you—and just to think, I missed on the second question after all . . . . This is bath night [whatever that meant, I really don't know] and again I must close in a hurry. You may say I'm always in a hurry; but, dear diary, this is the life at CBI. I received no mail today, and must say I missed it, it does me so much good to hear from home. I think we are going to the Ward's home tomorrow afternoon to make candy.*

Then a few pages later, after she tells about the fudge they made at the Ward's house which turned out like a malted milk shake, "Miss Uzon" writes this candid prayer, intended, I'm sure, only for God and the pages of her diary,

> *Dear Lord, Oh my precious Heavenly Father, how I love Thee —but oh how my heart aches, when I think of my many failures, my many weaknesses. Truly I marvel and wonder how You can love one such as me. Dear Lord, no one knows me like*

You do, no one knows my heart, my soul, my wants, my needs, my desires as you do. Oh that I could put away forever the thoughts of my mind and heart that are displeasing to you. I would so like to live to please You wholly, yes wholly, that nothing, no nothing, dear precious Lord will come between Thee and me. That I will live always to please thee, "A woman after Thine own heart."

Dear Saviour, Thou seest that I am unable to do as my soul is want to do—wilt Thou not fill me with Thine dear strength and give me power to live the Christ-like life? Stamp thine own image deep on my heart. Make me a blessing to someone today.

Even so, Lord, because you have first loved me—help me to show to Thee, in service, my love for Thee. It is nothing, yet what I have, oh God, I give to thee.

One day later, in her diary, she writes about the troubled day her mouth and outspoken honesty has caused her.

Dear Diary,

Friday, the 27th, 1928, and never a day like this again . . . . The sun has set with its glorious rays of beautiful colors. The sun set on this day also, never again to rise for another such day, and so it is with my thoughts and my words, actions and deeds.

Today's deeds and words have set and they can never be brought back.

The mean words I have spoken can never be taken back, my mean ways cannot either. They have gone with today. So, I pray not for today—as it is well nigh past—but I pray for tomorrow. Dear Lord, somehow make me and form me in Thine own image. Let me say things You would say and let me do the deeds You would do. Help me make tonight, after Thine pattern, even while I'm resting in the quiet still hours of the night, and help me that, when I awake in the morning, Thy strength will be resurrected in me and that Thy glory will shine in and through me—for others.

Mother didn't reveal the details of her conversation, and I don't know the exact words she used. But I do feel, from her diary, that the Hungarian candor in her had controlled her mouth, and obviously she was terribly upset that what she had said had hurt someone else. She was already experiencing the down side of her unguarded honesty—especially as it related to other people.

About this time, Mother's diary contains a number of glowing sentences about "Mr. M" or "Mr. C." She seems quite enchanted by this young man (Clifford Andrew Miller). However, she's not about to give up her calling to Africa by falling in love with anyone—much less a man who has been called as a missionary to China. On the other hand, this Mr. C has simply swept her off her feet, if by nothing else but the gifted way he plays the violin at chapel services. She writes,

It's getting late, dear diary, and I must close, in a hurry. Oh, yes, I must not forget—the violin solo—It was splendid— beautiful—oh, how I wish I could play and pour out my feelings thus—"

And then her smitten heart adds,

I also wish my dreams would come true.

In the next entry, she writes that "Mr. M" asked her, after breakfast in the dining room, if he could write her a note. (That's the way they did things in Bible school in those days . . . Who knows why?) The predictable effect on Miss Uzon is as old as love itself. All day she finds she can't concentrate in classes, she can't study, she can't practice the piano, she can't have a good time with a group of friends after supper. So she wrote,

After the evening at Vandervort's home ended, I came back to my room and my "note" was waiting for me. Without taking off my hat or coat I sat down and began to read. I enjoyed it very much—but somehow it made me feel heavy and sad.

I got down to pray—but couldn't. All night I tossed to and fro —didn't sleep much.

Went down to breakfast this morning and asked him if I should answer his note. He said, "Yes." [Again, don't ask me why he had to ask her or she had to ask him—it was just done that way.] So there was another worry. What to write and how?

I had a headache or something—missed my Prophecy class, lay down for that period. Then, after dinner I didn't practice the piano but wrote my note.

I'm rather ashamed of it now but it's too late. I hope he doesn't think I'm terrible, but I wrote just what was on my heart—and I could have written more. I still have some things I want to say—trust I will have nerve enough to do it soon.

Knowing her ability to write freely what was on her heart and of her honesty before God, herself and others, I feel certain the personal contents of their "notes" dealt with the one major flaw in their relationship—the fact that the directions of their lives were headed toward opposite parts of the world.

In one place in her diary she says of "Mr. M":

If God desires to send him to China no one can stop Him. I told L.P. about it, Lillian and Kay—they seemed to encourage me somewhat—and I'm not discouraged for if it is His will—He will bring it to pass. I did ask God, though, to please keep me out of love affairs until the right time comes! I know He will. Yes, I am praying for Mr. M. I want Jesus to have His own sweet way in our lives. And if Jesus sees best to send him to China, I want to be willing—for if China needs him more—I am willing to go alone, without him, to my home—in Africa. I'll let him go where the Master has need of him.

Father, in Thy sweet hands I lay this case. Weave out Thy gracious will and bring it to light. Show us each the way. Give us assurance and sanction it. Let us know Thy way and, then, give us grace to go that way.

Three days later her heart is soaring. Joyously she writes in her diary, for obviously she's head over heels in love with "Mr. M." Now she's letting her emotions get serious. In fact

she left his initial of "Mr. M" or "Mr. C" and now uses just
"C" for Clifford . . .
So, she wrote,

Dear Diary,

*This has been a happy day—a day of victory! This noon we
changed tables and "C" is in my dining room!*

*I asked Mr. Sumrall to call "C" and tell him I want to speak to
him. He did and we met at 1:45 pm in the dining room. Had a
lovely talk with him—he told me he cared for me—it thrilled
me!*

*But we are praying about the mission field the Lord would have
him go to—we'll pray each night from 10:00 to 11:00 pm. We
will pray for one another—we're brought together, to the throne
of grace, in that way. Though we are far apart—we are drawn
and brought nigh in prayer."*

A few nights later, and again because of her frankness
with God, she is not afraid to write about the wide range of
her feelings. One senses that she's not worried about God's
shrinking back from her in horror, or telling her that she
ought to "trust Him" more. However, it's apparent that no
matter how happy she is with Mr. C and how united she
feels with him in prayer, she guesses that the handwriting
on the wall is beginning to spell out a rather disheartening
message.

Now, in her diary, quite like most of us, she vacillates
between two avenues of prayer. One moment she leaves the
problem in God's capable hands, peacefully entrusting him
to care for it. The next moment she pulls back the problem
and struggles with the enormous load of unwanted yet continuous worry. Physically she feels sick with the dread. Her
worst fear scenario is that God will send "Mr. C" to China
and her to Africa. This terrible dichotomy plunges her usual
"positive thinking" and cheerful personality downward
into a new and scary emotion: depression. I sense from her
diary that she has never encountered depression before,

57

and she is stunned by the unexpected effects produced by her dark thoughts. She puzzles over these new, anguishing feelings . . .

Dear Diary,

This has been one of those blue days. Oh, Lord, what must I do to get away from these spells? Give me grace to stand it, if it must come.

Dear Lord, I long to be in such a place in Thee, where I will only desire that which is Thy sweet will. Wipe out all fleshly desires—for I want my life to be pleasing to Thee alone. Please Jesus, dear Jesus, fill me with You. Shine in me and make me a blessing—not for myself, but to others.

They tell me I mustn't wish to die—but what is this life anyway compared to heaven? That's the place that Jesus went to prepare for me. I have a right, a blessed claim, a share in that beautiful place.

In the following days, on the pages of her diary, Miss Uzon repeatedly shares her frustration about herself with God. In undisguised openness she reveals that her faith is going through its first real testing time. She exposes her heart to God. She ponders the merits of giving up her "dearest" person for Africa, and she pours out her baffling emotions about being in love for the first time.

As I was in the midst of reading her words, I tried to imagine what it must have been like for a twenty-two-year-old Christian woman in those times. I wondered about the cultural and social climates, and what pressures the peer groups put on each other? Mostly I wanted to know which issues Christians felt were most important? What did they strongly care about? These thoughts and others rattled the cages of my mind so vigorously that I got out our encyclopedias, books and other research material to take a better look at the people and times of my mother's world in 1928.

I found that historically and religiously it was a most intriguing time. Society's attitudes gave off a distinctly divided ambience. There seemed to be a polarization of two decidedly different life styles in the country. One well established at this time was, as the historians termed it, "American Protestant Middle Class," and this was Marion's (and most everyone's at Central Bible Institute) comfort zone.

It was interesting to discover that beside Protestants many Catholics and Jews took comfort in the same goals and values. Many people believed in the hard work ethic, with its need for everyone, men, women and children to be continuously industrious. They put a high priority on being thrifty. They doggedly pursued perfection and, last but certainly not least, they characteristically placed great emphasis and insisted on the importance of "being known" as a person with high moral standards. All these attitudes and, of course, many others were seen as absolutely necessary to maintaining personal integrity. They were also essential and vital to achieving social and economic success and acceptance.

However, the new kid on the block in the 1920s was an unruly and undisciplined fellow named "Roaring Twenties." He came on the scene wildly rebellious and was more than ready to kick down the solid doors of the old established houses of traditions and ethics. Many Christians like my mother, the professors, pastors and students around her, all faced an interesting and frustrating problem. Most of them couldn't and wouldn't embrace the attitudes of the Roaring Twenties. Certainly they could not kick off their beliefs or the sacred traditions of the church like a pair of worn out shoes. It was, in their words, a very "worldly" time, something they wanted no part of, yet they *were* alive in this world. Their battle came in trying not to be *of* the world, as the Scriptures pointed out, and still living *in* that world at the same time.

As I read historical accounts and commentaries of these times, my own personal observation is that in the 1920s Christians, in an effort to prove the validity of their belief systems, clung tenaciously to a carry-over idea from Victorian times. They listened to a Victorian message which made good sense to them. It went something like this: *"Proper people* and *Godly people* cover up or hide their real true feelings."* One of the most popular sayings was "Never air your dirty linen in public," meaning that you were to pretend in public that you were happy/clean/rich or right all the time.

So Christians probably felt they had little choice here. They couldn't very well join the opposition and accept a rebellious life style. The question was, how could they live and maintain their legalistic adherence to the law and their commitment to being perfect and holy and still daily live and work on this planet?

Most sermons being preached at that time included a theology that scared people to death. It was popularly entitled "hell-fire and damnation." And, it was clear that if you were not "saved and sanctified," victorious on all fronts, and a happy camper for God you were headed straight for the hot pit. This put a considerable strain on Christians, because no child of God was going to admit to having any thoughts or emotions that were less than simply holy and incredibly spiritual and joyous. No sir, not if they had a brain cell working in their heads.

I maintain, at this point in theological history, that the body of believers entered into a unique era of denial. They were almost obligated to keep hidden any dark sin or even uncomfortable thoughts or experiences. It was especially bad when they knew they fell short of being "dead to sin" because it forced them to respond to life in ways which demanded denial on their part. They were in a position which left them no choice but to deny they had any spiritual struggles, doubts or questions. They couldn't afford to let anyone see their brokenness or glimpse their genuine anguish. The best kept secret of their lives had to be their pent-up emotions of anger, disappointment or failure. They were programmed, as it were, to pretend that nothing was wrong—ever. They had to behave as if nothing was out of place or even painful; so, of course, that lead to pretending and acting out life on a daily basis as one *wanted* others to see it, rather than the way it really was. I think it was at this time in the 20th Century that we, as God's children, denied the unpalatable truth that sometimes life gives no answers. That even for Christians, terrible injustices happen and that life seems to have no rhyme or reason to it. Worst of all, Christians kept alive the denial which covered over man's most secret misery, that sometimes it appears that God is very silent, that he is hidden in a cloud and oh, how we long to see his face!

Perhaps some Christians kept up this kind of pretense and denial because they were afraid that if they admitted their unhappiness, or failures or (God forbid) their depression, then somehow that would be a very bad reflection on God. "It's just best," they reasoned, "to keep it all inside."

I personally believe that the lack of honesty and the denial factor in dealing with the realities of life are, then as now, one of the greatest hindrances to our healing and our wholeness on this curiously brutal yet glorious planet.

Of course, what fascinates me about my mother's diary is that I don't know how she ever broke through the great cover-up patterns of denial in the 1920s. I wonder, how did she manage to maintain her unequivocal honesty with God? It was certainly not in vogue for Christians, especially for women, to admit anything to anybody. And how did she keep the channels of her personal honesty within her own soul open and transparent? How did she do that, especially in light of the social and cultural mores of the church at the time?

Unaccountably, Miss Uzon set her sights on breaking through the pat configurations of denial in her days; and quite obviously in her writings on the pages of her diary, she succeeded in doing so. Perhaps it was her strong willed Hungarian genes which determined her passion to tell things as they really were. Who knows? For a certainty, on almost every entry in her diary she showed the unusual and rare dimensions of her honesty. In those times, her approach to God through prayer was in clear contrast with the denial theories which were prevalent back then. It seems she held nothing back from God.

I feel that for the rest of her life she continued this unrestrained openness with her heavenly father. She believed unequivocally that God loved her and she believed the Bible. Especially dear to her were the Psalmist's words which reported that while she was still being formed in her mother's womb, God planned out and scheduled all her days. She not only believed those words, but she acted on them as *her* own inheritance and her birthright as God's child.

Marion hid very little, as you can tell by the following excerpt. One can almost hear her fluttering heart as she boldly tells her diary about the realities of being in love with Mr. C. And she seems willing to trust, with all her might, that God is hearing her and understands her heart.

I was standing outside the dining room. Suddenly, he came toward me. He called me over and I met him. He told me there was something on his heart and he wanted to see me tonight after supper. I consented. We parted.

I went to my room quite excited and flustered. I must say, and even worried. Somehow I felt I knew what he wanted to see me about. Got down on my knees to pray—spent most of the afternoon that way. I could hardly wait for supper time to come, but when it did I could hardly wait for it to be over. I wasn't very hungry and I guess I forgot about others. After-supper came at last—and then the time went so fast.

He told me just how he felt. I guess he loves me, though he never told me so. We do want His best will in our lives.

Dear Lord, make me willing to let Mr. C go if it's Thy will. Reveal it to me. Oh, dear Lord, work in these few days as you've never worked before. Dear Lord, you know I love him. You know we can work for Thee better together—than single. Oh God, both of us seek to please Thee. If we love each other surely, Lord, you do not want us to part. If he is for me, You will not let him think he belongs in China. Make him see the need of Africa—bring it before him. I know it is not impossible with Thee. Dear Lord, grant me the desires of my heart—and I pledge to serve Thee all the days of my life. See my heart and answer accordingly. I'm so glad I don't have to make mention of it. You know just the condition and need I'm in.

It's almost 10:00 pm and I must stop, though I could write many other things. I am going to pray again, after 10:00 until God answers from Heaven.

[Signed]

Heart broken — sad and lonely

The next day, she wrote freely,

Dear Diary,

All day my thoughts dwelled upon the things spoken of last night. Got up before 7:00 am, dressed and had a season of prayer. Oh how prayer does give strength for the day. One hour of prayer at Jesus' feet will win victories over weeks and weeks of worry. I read in God's Word that worry is a sin — somehow I am subject to these awful spells and wish I could get away from it. How sweet it would be for me — not to worry, but simply to rest it in Jesus and let Him carry the burden for me . . . ."

What tickles me about these sober pages, even though they reveal my mother's inner agony between her call to be a missionary and her love of C, was the aim of her prayers to God about their unique quandary. I searched the pages of her diary and nowhere did I find her ever praying or even suggesting to God that the Lord make *her* willing to give up Africa and go to China with Mr. C. Her plea was steadfastly for God to make Africa very real to Mr. C and show him that that's where he was to go and be a missionary. I'll say this for her, she was one determined Hungarian lady.

There are some who would say Miss Uzon may have been praying "amiss"—or out of the will of God. But I think she firmly believed that since God loved her as his child, and was her dear father, she could feel free to advise him of the "desires of her heart." With great faith, even though she was unable to see *how* God was working, she remained confident that he *was* working. It was as if, at one point, she decided she would trust not only the troubling details of her life but even her dearest wishes to such a God. Her relationship with her heavenly father through prayer was direct, real and without masks or walls. She had no need to play cover-up games or hide her heart in denial from him who knew all about her. She continues her running dialogue with God and notes in her diary,

. . . of course, Mr. C.M. and I were together after supper at "free time"—until the lights blinked. My, but they seemed to blink earlier this night than other nights. I thought, "But no, it was because I was with _____."

We are still praying about _____ _____. [Here she left two blank spaces. It's not hard to imagine that the words were Africa and China.] God, I am confident, will work it out; and, if it may not be His will, I'm sure He will not let us fall and fail and ruin our lives. God is faithful and true to His children—Oh, that I could be true to Him as He is to me. I'm Thine, yea, wholly Thine. All that I have—take it and use it—for Thy glory in Africa.

Lord, thank Thee for the many blessings Thou has bestowed upon me and for the many dear Christian friends you have given me. Dear Lord, let me be a true pattern of 1 Corinthians 13—toward these and others. I thank Thee for Thy goodness and mercy and love towards me.

Make me fit, at least somewhat, to go out and tell this wonderful story of Your love. To tell of this Great Lover of our souls who has truly won my heart. Oh, tongue of mine, if you ever speak, you must praise God, you must let your light shine for Jesus, you must let your lips sing of His goodness and you must let others see Jesus in you!

Oh, diary, I could tell you of these wonderful times together—My Lord and I—I would but I can't express—I can't tell. The nearest to it I can say is—indescribable—it's heaven—it's glory.

This eve I saw my dearest. He looked so blue. It made me feel sad to see him so but I'm going to pray for him before my head

*touches the pillow and I know my dear Redeemer will help him
and meet his needs.*

*By faith I reach out and take what the Lord has for us. Not for
self, Lord, but for Thee and Africa.*

But the days dissolve into weeks and still nothing changes
except that Marion and Mr. C are more in love than ever.
Amazingly they remain completely dedicated to going their
separate ways—Mr. C to the mission field of China and she
to Africa.

Then the "ultimate honesty" with God begins to be seen
on the pages of my mother's diary. She copies out poems
about heaven and song lyrics like the words of this old
hymn,

> "Oh, I want to see Him,
> look upon His face,
> There to sing forever
> of His saving grace.
> On the streets of glory let me
> lift my voice,
> Cares all past, home at last,
> ever to rejoice."

and underneath these words she writes,

*The song above expresses a little of my feelings and desires. I
long to be with Jesus. Perhaps I'm too selfish and am trying to
shrink from my duty—to get away from these testing times and
trials that must come to every Christian. I feel as though I'm a
coward—and of course I am—but oh, how I want to go home to
heaven. How I long to see Him—and gaze upon Him—and be
filled with rapturous wonder amazed at His glory and beauty.
But this thought comes to me: No cross, no crown. Perhaps if I
went to heaven and missed these sad heartaches, I would also
lose my crown, and then I'd have nothing to bestow at His feet—
no fruit, not even leaves, but a dried up twig I would be—of no
use on this earth and, of course, no use there. So again, dear Lord
I pray, stir me, stir me, stir me. Give me power every hour to be
true to Thee.*

But, oh, I am heartbroken tonight—I'm wounded very deeply and, oh, how it aches. I cannot look to friends or dear ones here to comfort me. I must find a solace in the Lord—in the secret place of prayer. So I went to God, to Him who knows my frame. I told Him all. There was not a thing I didn't tell Him, and those things that I could hardly utter. God looked down into my naked heart and saw it all—nothing is hid from Him.

Now I want to go and go quickly—I want my life to wear out for Thee. Depart, oh depart, my wishes, my desires. I cannot have them—so why do I cherish them in my heart? Take them out, oh God. Take them away for it is eating my life away.

I have no desire to remain here—I want to go and do Thy bidding—finish it and let me hurry off to be with Thee—safe in the arms of Jesus. There'l be no sorrow there—no pains, no tears and, thank God, no disappointments and heartaches . . . .

Somehow, I can't give up . . . I think I see a faint light streaming steadily through the black clouds. Give me faith, oh God, to hold on in prayer . . . .

She was at the place so many millions of Christians have been (myself included)—that terribly dark place where pain is of such an incredible magnitude that it pushes our bodies and souls into the only corner left. We begin to fantasize about the relief a pain-free Heaven would bring, how utterly peaceful it would be to lie down and rest in God's bosom, and how ecstatic it would feel to leave agony behind—never to have to deal with it again! When pain and suffering become our prison cell on this earth, then, like all prisoners, we dream of nothing but escaping. While we cannot bring ourselves to take our own lives, still we pray for God to rescue us, to bring about our death, in whatever way he chooses, so we can leave the pain behind. Oh, how we pray that somehow he'll whisk us away from the unutterable throes of pain to the unspeakable glories of heaven! I believe my mother was in that corner, all right, and perhaps for the first time. I'm sure she was stunned at her capacity to hurt. She prayed,

66

Dear Lord, is it possible that my heart which has been broken can be healed? Oh, my God, why hast Thou forsaken me? Why art Thou so far from helping me? You know that to Thee only do I look for guidance and to Thee only do I come for help. It almost seems to me as though heaven and earth were against me.

Never, no never, will I forget the night I cried for mercy to Thee —pleading with Thee, never, to never allow things such as these to come into my life—they cause such heartache. Dear Lord, I prayed with my whole heart that day—I pleaded and pleaded over and over again until I thought surely, God has answered and will help and save me from it all. But here I am tonight, dear Lord, feeling cursed—yes, cursed. Thou seest that I am. I cannot hide it from Thee—neither can I make believe, for Thou knowest.

What does it all mean, dear Father? Why has this thing come upon me? I did not ask for it, I did not wish for it, I did not desire it. I told you, Lord, that if you wanted me to go into the heart of Africa I would go. I feel the same this moment. Though perhaps Africa may force me to make the sacrifice—almost too dear to me. Yet, if God wants it this way, I'll give up my dearest possession on earth, Mr. C, for Thee and Africa.

The next entry tells of a missionary convention held at the college—complete with "splendid music and a fine orchestra." Evidently she was quite struck by two "most touching messages," both given by single women missionaries. One from China and the other from Africa. She writes,

After that last message my heart failed me! "Could I go to Africa alone?" was the heart searching question. Will I ever stand it all alone?—as that dear missionary (may God bless her)—did. In the heart of Africa—no friends, no loved ones and not even a white man around? Could I go? This question is not settled in my heart yet . . . . But God knows my heart.

If I'm to go to Africa alone—with no one to help me—no human love to sustain me, with no arm of flesh to lean upon, God knows all about it. If it must be that I go to Africa without a companion, God will have to give me more strength—more of

*His grace—more of His love and more of Himself. If I will have
no human flesh to help me—God knows I will have to look to
Him more often—and trust Him fully. If this is your dear will,
Lord, make me willing to give up all.*

The next day Mr. C, obviously having heard the same
speakers at the conference, wrote a note to Marion about his
feelings. She doesn't reveal his words, but one can quickly
guess that Mr. C did *not* say he was giving up China to go to
Africa with her. She appears weary and very puzzled by it
all. Truly she desperately wants to get on with her life's
calling to go to Africa; so, like the Old Testament prophet
Elijah, she begs God to "hear and answer." She writes,

*I received a letter from Clifford [ah, finally she writes out the
letters of his name] this noon. I hurried up to my room just as
fast as I could—though not very anxious to read it for I felt I
knew what the note contained.*

*After reading it a great lump came into my throat. My heart
fairly pounded—and my hands and knees shook with weakness.
My cheeks blushed. Once I read it—oh, its almost unbearable.
What shall I do?*

*One help and one help only was in view—Jesus would help
me. So in my haste and heartsick condition I went into the
closet—shut the door behind me (the first time in my life that
I can remember). Lifted up my hands and cried, "Oh! God! You
must help me. Work it out!" This was all I could say—It was
not a pretty prayer—but it came from my inmost being and
truly I hope that the dear Lord will receive that cry and send
the answer back from heaven.*

*Lord, I can't go on much longer in this condition. You must help
me. I must have Thee.*

Her prayers over this were usually boiled down to three
words—*Work it out.* Two days later, she says,

*Wrote a letter to C (my answer to his). How I enjoy reading them
[Clifford's letters], even though it's heartbreaking. I'm so sorry*

68

I'm to be blamed for all this. I wish we never would have met —for it has been nothing but heartaches since.

But God knows all about this —His way is best. Our ways are not His ways —There is a purpose in this. It is for our good. "All things work together for good. But He knoweth the way that I take —when He hath tried me, I shall come forth as gold" (Job 23:10).

Evidently she was able to leave dealing with her Mr. C and the confusing dilemma in God's hands to *"work it out"* because directly under the passage of scripture from Job, her spirits seem to revive and Miss Uzon records,

Had a limburger cheese party tonight —Grace S., Silvia Davidson, Dick, Lil, E.D., Jenny Hildred, Dot and I. Hildred played dead —so it caused a little trouble. We're always getting into some kind of trouble.

And, two days later she's still in fine spirits as she writes,

Had a fine day —went out and played volleyball. Some of the boys came over and joined in with us. Other boys came over and just watched the thrilling game. I had the best time.

However, God has not yet "worked it out." Nothing is settled involving her love for Clifford or about her call to Africa, so she writes,

. . . Three weeks have now gone by. I am happy to be here because I know Jesus has placed me here.

Where I shall go after graduating I cannot say —but that Jesus has a plan for me —somewhere and that somewhere will be heaven to me —for where Jesus is —'tis Heaven there.

Then, since still nothing has changed and God has not given her direction, she comes up with her own therapeutic suggestion for peace of mind. She pens a prayer about Clifford,

My dear most Precious Lord,

I am going to be a prayer warrior. I am going to pray through for Clifford, for his work and for lost souls.

Often I have wondered of what help I can <u>ever</u> be to him. The answer was made real today: <u>Be a prayer warrior.</u> Stand behind C with the ropes of prayer, bring in souls through prayer. The Lord will bless and use him—only through prayer.

Oh God, this is my oath before Thee. Keep me true to my word to Thee. Oh, dear Lord, you know I <u>cannot,</u> no never can I do this of myself—but You help me to pray through for him—the only one for whom I have a <u>true</u> love in my heart. God, my dear Father, I love Clifford—yet if ever he is mine and I am his—<u>Be Thou</u> only and always <u>first.</u> Thou has first place in my love. First of all because you gave Clifford to me. Second, I love Thee and want to be faithful to Thee <u>all</u> the days of my life.

It's amazing, for even though no solution and no answer comes, Miss Uzon remains transparent with the Lord. She continues her honesty with him. She questions, doubts, and asks "Why?" and then regains her sense of mission, all on the pages of this diary. It's easy to see that if she put so much on paper, there was probably still more honesty within her that she never wrote out. But over and over she pours out the twin realities of her life—her love of God and her personal hurts.

Many things have happened in my life these past few short months. The burden seemed so heavy at times that I thought I would die. Why—Why—Why—is the question in my mind and heart—but no response is given to my aching heart.

Someday we will understand it all! Have you prayed about it? Yes, Lord. Oft as I go to and fro, on life's busy road, I find that I'm holding conversation with an unseen friend.

"Work it out Lord." "Have Thine own way Lord." "Do it <u>now</u> Lord." Have these cryings of mine been going to the throne of grace—all in vain?

No, never! The answer is near, it must be on its way. Jesus, the great defender, my attorney, never lost a case. He will not lose mine.

Great was Miss Uzon's trust of God! And while she alternated between agony and ecstasy over her love of Mr. C and of her calling to Africa—even wishing and praying on some days that God would dispatch her heavenward, she hangs on to her childlike faith, believing God will "work it out," and often expressed it on the pages of her diary.

The incredible thing though is that when God *did* answer her prayers, He worked in a most unlikely, surprising, even beautiful way. God did not ask Mr. C to give up China or even to go with Miss Uzon to Africa. Nor did He require Miss Uzon to go to Africa alone without Mr. C. No, God acted like God, coming up on their blind side, in his own time, doing the unusual, the original, and designing the thing they never anticipated or imagined. God allowed Marion and Clifford to simply fail their major physical tests. For the rest of their lives they smiled and talked of the intriguing way God had "worked it out" and how he dealt with them, remembering how simple the solution had been: Two failed physicals! So neither could go to China or to Africa. The Lord unfolded his plan for their lives and led them to begin their ministry by becoming pastors to a little congregation in Saginaw, Michigan. After graduating and being released from the foreign fields of service, they married and began what would be the entwining of their lives together in ministry to others for the next thirty-five years.

All through her life, as far as I can tell, Miss Uzon never lost her Hungarianness, especially in regards to being honest with God, herself and others.

Thirty years after her days in Bible college, Marion Uzon Miller, Pastor Miller's wife, wrote in one of her little note books a short unfinished piece on honesty. Here again, she writes about her reasons for being honest with God. She entitled it,

Learn to be completely honest. Be still, for in silence you can't escape yourself. God doesn't like false faces. He likes us just as we are. I believe He longs for us to be honest with Him — so He can heal the fracture of our souls, apply the oil of gladness and comfort us with the balm of Gilead.

We should bring the whole, the sum total of ourselves up to God. Even bring our whole personalities to God.

God can't do much with the parts of our minds and souls we have hidden. He doesn't go behind the locked doors of our life. But when we do open to Him and are truly honest with Him — He comes in with all His love and frees us. God appreciates honesty. Look at the story of the raising of Lazarus. Martha, particularly was bluntly honest. She said to Jesus, "He died and it's your fault." Then later when Jesus tells them to take away the stone from the tomb, Martha says, "It's been four days and by now he smells."

We have to honestly face the stench in us if we want resurrection.

My mother knew she could trust God with her hidden hurts, her most secret thoughts and her inner desires. She felt she could bring everything into the open with God. She had discovered a truth of great magnitude when she realized that we have to "honestly face the stench in us if we want resurrection." She understood that there could be no healing for a wound if you denied the wound existed.

The lesson of being honest with God was taught to me by mother's continued example. I always felt, by her conversation and her responses, that she wore no masks with God even though she believed that honesty with God could be at times the sharpest of scalpels. From her I caught the idea that reality did the best job of lancing the hidden infection of a boil. The scalpel, though, in God's gentle hands, did not destroy or kill. On the contrary, it restored and brought healing.

While my mother's spirits were generally upbeat and she could find delightful reasons for beginning again and trusting God with painful issues, still, her honest practical side kept her acutely attuned to one very undeniable fact. She seemed to understand better than most of us, that often life on earth was more hell than heaven.

Reality, that sharp scalpel, was what she termed living the "crucified life"—meaning that she would not deny or minimize the pain part of being a Christian. She would accept it for what it was, a part of a Christian's life, a necessary part for growing and making progress. She wrote years later,

> *Your being a German or a Hungarian makes inevitable certain habits of the mind, a certain type of temperament of the soul. But, your being a Christian makes inevitable a "crucified life."* *John 10:17-18, John 12:29*

No denial here. She knew about the honesty needed to survive and to heal in this world. She also had a great grip on timing as well as honestly revealing ourselves to God. She wrote in a later notebook,

> *Christians today, as always, are waiting on God to answer their prayers. Many have waited long and have doubted God has heard. Others have become offended, especially when God has said "No," or worse yet, "Not now," and have charged God foolishly. When Job's whole life went out the window the scripture says, "In all of this Job did not sin or charge God with wrong" (Job 1:22, RSV).*
>
> *God's waiting room is the most tiresome and unpleasant place in our Christian experience. We do not like delays or denials, for hasn't God said, "Ask, and it shall be given you"? (Matt. 7:7) God has reasons for delays. Some He will reveal to us, others we may never know, but one thing we know for certain—God never makes a mistake!*

I realize I've written a great deal on these pages about honesty with God, *but that's where all genuine honesty begins*. We start by being intimately honest with our maker, with no fear of recrimination and with no worry that whatever we dredge up will shock God into abandoning us.

This kind of straight forwardness with God helps, maybe even forces us to be honest—not only with him—but with ourselves as well . . . no hiding, no cover up, no denial, but a sincere desire to live life as realistically as humanly possible.

After we are honest with God and with ourselves—what about honesty with others? What about our relationships with others? Another part of the gift of honesty, from my inheritance, was the training and the teaching that honesty with others had the powerful effect of destroying or healing, depending upon how we used it.

There is a vast difference between cruel honesty and kind honesty. It is obvious to me that even though Miss Uzon was only twenty-two years old when she wrote out these thoughts, she had a well-developed awareness of how opposite cruel and kind honesty could be. Several places in Mother's diary reveal this conflict. She paid a dear price for learning about that difference in cruel, devastating honesty and kind, nourishing honesty in relationships with others. One recording in her diary starts with this declaration:

I have tried so hard to be good lately. But all in vain. Last Thursday I was in my room darning "Mr. C's" socks and really didn't want anybody to know about it. A knock was heard at my door. Quickly I hid my darning, but Hildred noticed that something was up. I didn't want to tell her but my roommate Dot told. For a moment I felt sad, then peeved (not angry, for I can't be with my roommate Dot) but oh, of course an argument began —and as usual, I was in the wrong. I was wicked about it.

I have tried oh so hard to be loving and kind—an example of a Christian who is patterned after 1 Cor. 13, but I failed.

Oh, dear Lord, will I ever be in such a position, in such a place with Thee where I may not be afraid to open my mouth—but be confident that Thou art in me and living the life? "Not I but

Christ liveth in me." Though often my dear friends would never think so!

Many years later one of the letters I found in my mother's folders marked "Current Correspondence" verified her lifelong quest for kind honesty. It graphically pointed out that, from the days of her journaling in her diary throughout her almost sixty years, she had a firm grip on understanding her own vulnerability with honesty. From one particular letter before me, I know that a few weeks before her death my mother had been her usual outspoken self to a board member of Dad's church. Apparently she'd voiced her feelings and opinions at an annual business meeting. It was definitely one of those meetings where women were supposed to close their minds and shut their mouths. I can also tell, from her letter, that the man—both angry and bitter—resigned from the board and left the church, but not before he acrimoniously denounced "Pastor Miller's wife" to the entire congregation.

Mother, in her usual way, had been the first and the fastest to recognize what she'd done. She seemed to fully understand how her Hungarian-quick tongue paved the way for chaotic contention. She was also willing to "own" her responsibility for her words and to admit to being wrong. So, in her letter to this unhappy man, she speedily set about righting her own wrongs and began reaching out to heal their broken relationship. I'll never forget the admiration I felt for my mother as I read her words. They revealed so much of her inner character and integrity. With words, both humble and honest, she had written to the man in one part:

Oh, dear sir, forgive me if I have been a stumbling block in your life.

Then, after pouring out her heart and taking the responsibility for the problem, she caught sight of the real issue at stake between them and wrote,

Even if you don't come back to our church, though I wish you would, forgive me and serve Christ in another church. You are so needed for God's service and He needs workers like you!

In view of the fact that I was acquainted with the man in question, and not terribly fond of him, it's probably best that resolving the problem with him was not left in my hands. I certainly would have handled it in a vastly different way than my mother. (Actually, after I read Mother's whole letter, my desire to push a fat sock into his mouth was one of my *nicer* thoughts.) My mother's choice of attitudes here was simply astounding. Obviously, because of the level of reality, I could tell that she'd learned her lessons well regarding the pitfalls of her Hungarian honesty.

The letter itself, much less her sound reasoning and meekness of heart, were more than impressive—especially in view of the fact that when she wrote the letter she knew she was dying. I know now that strength and energy were oozing out of her as she struggled in the losing fight with advanced breast and lung cancer. Yet there was no trace of self-pity in her letter to this man. In fact, she didn't even mention her illness. Nor did she refer to her physical state to gain sympathy, or to prove she was right. She didn't even try to have the last word. No, there was none of that, even though this was undoubtedly one of her last letters to someone other than her children.

I believe, in this letter and with classic style, Marion Uzon Miller took care of some unfinished business—dealing honestly with God, herself and others. Straightforwardly she addressed what she believed to be the real issue at stake here: the important need to encourage this man to go on with his life. She was looking at the man through eyes of love. Fervently she wished and prayed that he would enjoy being the man God had intended him to be.

If I boiled down the lessons of my inheritance on honesty from my mother's diary, notebooks and papers and added my own recent experiences, the essence of my learning could be summed up in this way. First, I must be honest with God. There's absolutely no point in attempting to hide anything from him. In Psalm 139 the Psalmist writes,

O Lord, You have examined my heart and know everything about me. You know when I sit or stand. When far away you know my every thought. You chart the path ahead of me, and tell me where to stop and rest. Every moment You know where I am. You know what I am going to say before I even say it (Psalm 139:1-4, TLB).

So, if God does indeed know everything about me, my thoughts (both good and wicked) and the words I'll say, and even when I'll say them, then I must not act the fool before him. I must not pretend he doesn't see my real motives or the darkest inner sanctums of my heart. He does, yet he still loves me.

Truth and honesty must be quite important to God, for why else did the Psalmist write,

Mercy and truth have met together. Grim justice and peace have kissed! Truth rises from the earth and righteousness smiles down from Heaven (Psalm 85:10,11, TLB).

I strongly believe that God loves our transparency with him.

Secondly, I must be honest with *myself.* I need to guard against clothing my ego with the glittering image of denial and cover-up. I gain nothing from trying to impress myself with the idea that I'm right, I'm perfect and I'm whole.

For, in truth, I must candidly admit that I am what I am —a vulnerable person, broken and needing heaven and earth's love, forgiveness, restoration.

Thirdly, I must be honest with *others.* And here comes the very tricky part about honesty, for to be honest with others we must be conscious of hidden agendas, and active avoidance of subtly dangerous abusive ways. If I am going to practice honesty with others then I need to know a whole lot about my psychological anatomy and the categories of honesty. Let me start with the most negative one first: *Cruel Honesty.*

Cruelness in honesty happens when I tell the *truth* about myself, but it is really aimed as a put down to you, or to someone else. It's truth, yes, but when I practice cruel honesty my motive is intended to elevate myself above you. It's "truth" contrived to make me look infinitely better than you. It's a type of "honesty" which one must avoid as one would a highly infectious disease.

It's the exhausting sport of our times, that of truthful one-upmanship. Bragging and putting myself right up there next to Mother Teresa, especially when I look down my spiritual nose at you and say, "I get up at 4:30 every morning to spend an hour with the Lord in prayer and Bible reading." (Those of you who know me personally know I'm a night person, and the above line was made up, right here on the spot, as I wrote. But, you get my point, I'm sure.) The implied meaning here is that if *you* don't get up at 4:30 every morning you're spiritually a second class citizen, while I'm *first* class.

Cruel honesty is also that look of shocked disbelief which spreads slowly across my face while you're telling me that your greatest fears just came true, and I respond with "my truth" and say, sanctimoniously, "Well, *my* kids would *never* do *that!*"

Cruel honesty occurs the second you tell me that the circumstances of your life are disintegrating as we speak, and I offer you a crumb of "true" advice off my well-filled plate by saying, "Well, if you *wanted* to—you *could* work at your problem and trust God to do a miracle."

Cruel honesty is also that sick way of excusing my own bad manners and behavior or my rude comments with a twisted brand of truth. Say I've embarrassed you or said something very inappropriate, and I cover up my behavior by using cruel honesty. I say, "Hey, what's the matter with you? I'm just being myself. Open and honest, and I can't help it if you don't like it. I tell it like I see it, and that's just the way I am!"

However, the above examples of cruel honesty pale in the light of the most deadly type of honesty. That's the cruel honesty which happens when I tell the truth, as I know it, *about you* and it's totally destructive. The truth utterly annihilates your character, your reputation or your integrity. I can hear my mother giving me a quote from Proverbs which meant so much to her—"Self-control means controlling the tongue! A quick retort can ruin everything" (Proverbs 13:3, TLB).

Let's try this fictitious scenario on for size:

You attend a small prayer group of women and, after the leader opens the session with a devotional, she then invites everyone to present their prayer requests. Several women share their needs and then one member of the group raises her hand and speaks, "I think we should pray for Joann."

For a moment you and everyone else just sits there, waiting for a little more clarification. You know Joann. Well, in fact, you saw her the day before yesterday and she looked and sounded fine. Was she all right? Tentatively, you ask, "Why does she need prayer?" Another woman questions, "Is Joann sick, or one of her kids?"

The one who made the request replies, "Well, no . . . they're all fine. But, I just *know* we should pray for Joann. She needs our prayer support."

The atmosphere in the room grows thick with the fog of speculation as each woman searches her mind for any clue about Joann's needs. Then one woman makes an observation, and, aiming it at the woman who brought up Joann's name, says, "Pastor preached on Sunday about the necessity of praying *specifically*. So you need to tell us what's wrong, *exactly*, with Joann so we don't pray 'amiss.'"

"Well, I'm not sure I should share this," comes the answer, and it's accompanied by a tight-lipped silence which does nothing for the group but drive them crazy. So they press her for details in earnest. "What do you know about Joann that we don't?" comes the general consensus of minds. And, of course, by now even the leader is dying of righteous curiosity. So, with great diplomacy, she says, "Perhaps you can tell us what prompts your concern for Joann. And we'll be sure to keep it confidential."

Now the woman who made the request in the first place straightens a bit in her chair and, knowing she has everyone's undivided attention, she mentally walks to center stage and begins her *honest* declaration of truth.

"Well," she says dramatically, "I think Joann is having some problems—but I don't know. I'll just tell you what I *do* know. Joann's husband, George, is our church's maintenance man. Now, every Tuesday night he cleans the church from 7:00 to 9:00 P.M. But also, at that time on Tuesday night, Myrtle always practices the organ, and the two of them are here together all evening."

The group waits for any other tidbit of information but the woman fiddles with a loose strand of hair at the back of her head and sincerely states, "I'm just telling you the truth about a potentially dangerous situation, and I think we ought to pray for Joann."

What's transpired here is that one woman has, indeed, told the truth. For it is completely true that George *does* clean the church the same night as Myrtle practices the organ. But cruel honesty is being practiced and perpetuated here. Three people— Joann, George and Myrtle—have just experienced an *honest* assassination attempt on their character, their integrity and, yes, even their Christianity. Their chances for unblemished escape are not very good. *Yet, every word that was spoken was true.*

Sometimes we need to keep silent, even when we *know* the truth. Speaking about what "we know" may be that unthinkable cruel type of honesty which lays waste a person's soul. Actually it's so easily done that I fear few of us are aware of cruel honesty's devastation.

One tiny step away from cruel honesty is a more subtle form of destructive "truth telling." I call it *Qualified Honesty.* It has some interesting patterns and it also happens when we tell the truth about someone else but with a slightly different twist. We begin well, but we end the sentence with our own negative qualifier which is based on our own honest opinion.

Qualified honesty has many devious ways to go, but here are a few sample phrases:

"I really love my pastor, but . . . I wish his wife was more friendly."

"Personally, I like her as a woman, but . . . she's sure let herself go."

"I wouldn't want to wish them any harm, but . . . I feel like after what they did—they deserve what they got."

"I don't want to contradict you, but . . . it wasn't $5.37, it was $5.99."

"I believe God's forgiven her, but . . . I sure can't."

"I'm not being judgmental, but . . . that was the dumbest choice she ever made."

"I can appreciate her talents, but . . . she sings flat."

"I'm not being critical, but . . . if my children did that, I'd sure let them know who's boss."

"I'm not sure if this is true or not, but . . . just between you and me . . . ."

Qualified honesty, as you can see, has truth combined with our own personal opinion. It's a precarious position to choose. If we practice qualified honesty on others, we almost always have to clothe ourselves in a judge's robe. The problem with this is that judging can never be our strong suit, mainly because we don't know *all* the facts; nor is judging *our* duty or prerogative. God did not die and leave the judging to us. So, qualified honesty is just about ninety-five percent malignant and has the power to send another human being to the terminal ward of the nearest hospital.

One of the most refreshing things about the gift of honesty is discovering that we can choose *which* type of honesty

we will speak as the language of our life. I was blessed to
have a mother who, despite her Hungarian outspokenness
and sincere and continued drive towards truth, learned (yes,
sometimes the hard way) that the only type of honesty she
wanted anything to do with was *Kind Honesty.* So deliberately and with a great deal of thought, she chose it. She
tenaciously tempered her predisposition to "tell it like it is"
so that she could practice kind honesty. I saw her do this
time and time again.

As I look back over Mother's diary and the short days of
her life, I see that she also repeatedly taught me that striv-
ing for kind honesty would ultimately pay rich dividends.

Defining kind honesty, I'd have to say, that it happens
when we reveal the truth about ourselves—even when, if
someone else said it, it might have hurt.

My mother told the whole truth (even the bad or painful
truth) about her *own* life, and remember that anyone who
has this kind of truthfulness is breaking the very solid rule
about telling *only* your good points and your strengths. I
feel she was most truthful and, believe me, this set her
apart from most people—because she told about her weaknesses, her faults, her mistakes, her erroneous thinking and
her own inadequacies.

How she laughed when she retold a story of driving to
the Los Angeles convention auditorium with her friend,
Dale Evans Rogers, who was to be the key note speaker at
an event there. Mother, who was raised without going to
the movies or other "worldly pleasures," had no idea of
Dale's celebrity status nor any real inkling of her high visi-
bility and fame. So, as they were driving into Los Angeles,
mother saw people waving at them from the cars in the next
lane, and she mistakenly assumed that they were waving at
her. She said later, "My, I'd been on that freeway many
times but I never saw people *that* friendly before. I was so
pleased I waved back at them." It wasn't until the trip home,
when mother accidentally saw Dale waving her little finger
in greeting to a whole load of little boys in the station
wagon next to them, that she realized all those people and

kids had been recognizing and waving at Dale . . . not at her. Funny thing.

Mother loved telling self-effacing stories about herself. I see it now as her most ingenious way of teaching me the real lessons about kind honesty and how very important it was to practice it.

Kind honesty happens not only when we tell the truth about ourselves, but it also happens when we reveal the truth about someone else *and our words about them are affirming.*

The woman in my made-up story who requested prayer for Joann could have practiced kind honesty had she said *nothing* to the group of women about the "truth" of Joann's life. But, let me hasten to add here, if the Holy Spirit whispers a name to you—and in your thoughts that name comes up again and again—don't waste any time. Pray for that one. Especially if there are no obvious clues to what that person's needs might be. This is the time to pray—not to publicly declare or try to figure out the "truth" of someone's situation.

Kind honesty is exactly that: *Kind.* Sometimes it's practiced best *behind* someone's back. Like that moment when you are in a group and an individual brings up someone's name and then proceeds to malign or even make insidious hints about that person. You are practicing kind honesty when you speak up and say, "I don't know if what you are saying is true, but whether it's true or not isn't the issue here. The truth, the real truth, is that she is my sister in Christ and I love her." Kind honesty affirms others, sometimes verbally and other times silently.

Much is finally being said nowadays about verbal abuse. My heart and my mother's teaching and training tell me that the gift of honesty is one gift that *must* be taken seriously. We can't get arrested for wounding or killing another human being with our words, so maybe that's one reason why we don't believe we are being abusive with our honesty. There is a real need for us, as children of God, to examine our motives and the intent of our hearts when we *speak* the truth. Willfully, as Christian men and women (Hungarian or not!), we must opt for nothing short of *kind* honesty . . . communicating in clear tones to the people of our world, the real language of God's merciful love.

We are given some wonderfully dear guidelines for kind Christian honesty in the scriptures. I'm positive they set the pace for my mother's basic truthfulness.

We are told,

To think about honest things. (Philippians 4:8)

To walk in honesty. (Romans 13:13)

To be willing in all things, to live honestly. (Hebrews 13:18)

And Jesus, in his parable about the seeds and soil, told us, "But the good soil represents honest, good-hearted people" (Luke 8:15 TLB).

Of course, these words of Jesus, probably sum it up the best. We all have inherited the gift of honesty. It's ready, here, and available for us. And when we choose kind honesty we do indeed become "honest, good-hearted people." People who are a delight to be around. People who make doing business with them a pleasure. People of character and sterling integrity. And most definitely people who, like my mother, are a credit to the name of Christianity.

Chapter 4

"Understated elegance, suggesting great wealth" . . . those words explicitly described the box I now held in my mind's eye. The gold foil paper wrappings, the slim silver ribbon tied with its single bow, intrigued me though seen only in my imagination. What treasure was hidden in this newest gift of my inheritance?

Carefully, I removed the paper, untied the ribbon and, even before I discovered the contents of this box, I caught a breath-taking whiff of familiar perfume. I wished that the fragrant scented bouquet rising from the gift would stay and envelope me forever.

I had inherited, in the den of my parents' house that sad, yet most unforgettable day, the gift of acceptance. Its heady aroma had announced its substantial eternal value. Actually, it wasn't just one gift or two, but three, all wrapped up in one word: acceptance . . . all mine to claim, mine to use and mine to pass on to my children and others.

Eagerly I reached down into the folds of the flower scented tissue paper and lifted out the first of the three gifts of acceptance. It was not by mere chance that the gift on top was rather clearly labeled "Acceptance of God." How like my mother's thinking to prioritize the gift of acceptance in this sequence.

Much of the legacy we leave behind to our children is determined by our heart's desire for them. When it came to my mother's longings and heart's desires for her children, the dreams and aspirations she held for us contained a multitude of arenas and included the full scope of life's encounters.

Since my children are grown and I now have the luxury of hindsight, I've come to appreciate my precious mother and the inheritance she left me. I think she was a genius in understanding the true mystique and character of motherhood. It's obvious that she chose the path in the role of a mother prayerfully and carefully. Clearly, she chose to avoid being a pushy "stage mother," fixing things, manipulating people and trying to control situations for her children. At the same time, she did not take a hands-off approach or hold herself aloof from us. We knew mother stood firmly, one thousand percent for us, cheering and urging us towards our goals. Additionally we knew, and I've not checked this out with my siblings, but we always understood that mother's highest and most pressing *spiritual* desire for us was that we would accept and invite the presence of God to live within us. She wanted every one, especially her children, to know and love God in a most personal way.

So, I understood that if she'd left me the gift of acceptance, she'd start with God—but I thought it went without saying, that I'd *already* "accepted God."

I'd become a "Christian" when I'd consciously and deliberately chosen to accept God's rich gift of eternal life. Mother, of all people, knew what a glorious difference this acceptance of Christ had made in my life's directions. Certainly she'd known and watched my stumbling ways along with occasional progress. So, why leave me the gift of acceptance, starting with my choosing to accept God? For a moment I thought, *Well, she probably wanted to re-emphasize the old truth about salvation being a gift from God, but that the gift would do no good unless we accepted it. After all, what good is a gift if the person you are offering it to refuses it?*

But, hey, my mother knew that my choice of becoming a child of God had changed my life inside and out for time present and for eternity. So, what was her point? Perhaps she realized, long before I did, how we tend to think of "accepting Christ into our hearts" as the one hundred year old Evangelical term puts it, as strictly that—*accepting Christ.* Period. When in reality it is much more. Much more.

As I contemplated these thoughts, I could hear mother,

Joyce-Honey, accepting Christ into your heart and life *does* take precedence over other types of acceptance, that's why it's first here—but don't stop with accepting God . . . there's more, much more! Push on, honey, expand your mind and your soul . . .

Even today, as I sit here writing and pondering that first gift on top of two others in the acceptance box, I recall how many times I've walked myself through this labyrinth of rationality. I've said, "Oh, yes, I've accepted God and he has forgiven me." But, then I've added the familiar words, "Yet, I can't seem to forgive myself." In the years I've been counseling, in person and through the mail, this is one of the most prevalent thought patterns I've heard verbalized.

We seem to be capable of handling and accepting the theory of God's forgiveness towards us. But we can't quite get it through our heads that when he provides forgiveness, he sees us as *forgiven*. We continue to refuse to forgive ourselves and do as Martha Snells Nicholson's line reads, "I made a whip of my *remembered sins* . . ." Why is it so hard to accept God's viewpoint of ourselves?

Ephesians 1:4 gives us the very best of concepts as to how *God* sees us. Do we just read these precious words, nod our heads in "doctrinal" agreement, but refuse to *believe* the truth—even when it's before us?

Long ago, even before he made the world, God chose us to be his very own, through what Christ would do for us; he decided then to make us holy in his eyes, without a single fault—we who stand before him covered with his love (TLB).

This verse is the essence of what my mother wanted me to understand about accepting God. It was a pivotal and critical concept in the acceptance gift she left. Simply put, I was to accept the way *God* sees me. Mother did indeed know I'd accepted Christ. Now she wanted me to grow in a different direction. I was to accept God's viewpoint and his picture of me. I was not to look through my own screen or the lenses of others . . . I was to look at myself through the eyes of God, seeing me as *he* sees me.

Think of it! When we ask God to come and live within us, he does. Graciously and mercifully he forgives our sins. Then, as Ephesians 1:4 describes the moment, we stand before God. We stand naked, as it were, for he has seen in, through, and past our being. He knows all our secrets and the frailty of our frame. But, there we stand—a new child of God, "*covered* with his love." One translation says of that same moment, ". . . that we might be holy and blameless in his sight, living in the spirit of love" (TCNT).

How dare we accept God as our Savior, accept his forgiveness, and then refuse to see ourselves as he sees us, thus refusing to forgive ourselves? If God decided to make us "holy and blameless" in his sight, by forgiving us—then we need to accept his opinion of us, as his children, and *see* ourselves as forgiven by him. How foolish we must appear—when one second we open wide the door of our hearts to God, ask him in, and them immediately slam it shut on our own personal forgiveness. It's the ultimate insult to God. It's saying to him, "Theologically speaking, I accept you; but actually there must be a loophole or two in your promise of forgiveness." No wonder acceptance of God was on the top of the stacked gifts in this box of my inheritance!

I've been thinking about how many times, over the years, I have refused to accept God's perceptions and appraisals of Joyce. How many times have I stubbornly clung to the false notion that I am in charge of my forgiveness? How often have I donned pride's invisible cloak and minimized the value of Christ's gift by announcing, "I cannot forgive or forget my sins . . . I *can't* forgive myself"?

My sagacious mother wanted me to know, while she was here and after she was gone, that I could trust God's forgiveness *even* to the ultimate point of self-forgiveness; that if I did forgive myself, I'd be able to run the race with a clear, confident conscience, and my feet would be free from the muddy guilt of remembered sins. She wanted me to know and to believe that I am God's child, and that he's forgiven me. I could hear her ask, "Joyce-Honey, tell me, assured of God's forgiveness—what more do you need to run the race set before you?"

A few months after my father's death, in 1987, my darling step-mother, Elizabeth, discovered a wonderful prize. She found some recorded tapes of my mother's Bible studies from 1963. On one tape, Mother was teaching a lesson on this very issue and was asking, "What do we do about forgiving ourselves and putting the past to rest?" Beautifully, yet simply she says,

Put yesterday where it belongs . . . in the past. *Release* yourself from its mortgaging grip. Repeat often to yourself the verse of Hebrews 10:17, when God assures us about yesterday's sins: "And their sins and iniquities will I remember no more."

In other words, when I am tempted to say, "Yes, but I can't forgive myself because, you see, I *know* me and what I've done," then I am to repeat Hebrews 10:17 and accept God's statement that he has forgiven and forgotten the sins and the failures of my yesterdays. Only when I forgive myself, and feel the freedom of that forgiveness, can I move on. It sounds easy to do and, in a way, it is—but nevertheless, forgiving myself still takes an act of my will.

Today I've savored the fragrant gift of the acceptance of God's forgiveness and his perception of me. There is a deep settled peace hovering around my soul each time I remember that he *can't* remember my sins. Nor will he hold them against me; and, while I don't have God's ability to forget, still—nowhere is it written that I have to hold those sins against myself, especially since our heavenly father doesn't. My mother's words, "Release yourself from yesterday's mortgaging grip," peal like angel bells in my heart and lift me to a higher plateau of understanding and, certainly, facilitate the healing of my memories.

I was eager now to see what the other gifts of acceptance would bring to my ever-growing stockpile of the legacy I'd inherited. Precipitously, and erroneously, I assumed that if my accepting God and his view of me was the top gift in the box, then surely *accepting others* was the very next one. Right?

Wrong.

The middle gift was not the important gift of accepting others but the seldom used gift of *accepting myself*.

I smiled, remembering my mother's gift of honesty, and thought, *I should have known*. Accepting others is not next . . . for one simple reason. Accepting *myself* has to happen first. I had to accept God and his forgiveness before I could accept myself. And I must accept myself before I can move on to accepting others.

Mother was an erudite thinker, a woman abundantly blessed with a vast supply of spiritual insight. I'd rather not get overly verbose about her gifts lest she start a rebellion and lead a heavenly insurrection at being eulogized on these pages as a saint (although I'd like to canonize her). The truth is, she was a an earthy, practical woman, yet somehow set apart . . . not of this world. She was an extraordinary human being, and I'm still learning and gathering gems of wisdom from the inheritance she left me in 1966.

Combined with her undistorted perception of reality, and a nuts-and-bolts common sense grasp of the practical, Marion Uzon Miller—even from her early days in Bible college—understood the immense value of accepting herself, her life, her dreams and her destiny.

But, I'm cognizant enough of Psychology 101A, people and myself, to know that accepting one's own inner self is no easy snap-of-the-finger-it's-done assignment. Nor is it accomplished by the ordinary garden variety type of determination and will power. So, when mother left me this second gift of acceptance, I gave it my full attention. I could feel the urgency and the importance of the lessons mother wanted to teach me about accepting myself . . . as God sees me, with no presumption of guilt or indebtedness.

I believe that in order to accept herself, Mother began by accepting God's version of her life's story; and, following the example God set for her, she followed suit and forgave herself. Then, moving on, she found that she did not have to spend a great deal of time dredging about in the muck and mire of introspection and an analysis of "the old Marion and the new Marion." Nor did she have to fret and fuss over her immediate or long term circumstances or God's divine calling for her life. Accepting all aspects of herself also freed her from what I believe are two of the most crippling phrases ever uttered in one's lifetime. The words that whine, "Oh, dear. . . . Poor me. This is so terrible, and it's only happening to me. . . . No one else." And the second one, a regret that's accompanied by so much pain, which cries, "Oh, God. If I'd only done . . . or said it differently."

I don't recall hearing my mother expressing either one of those fallacies of faith, and yet there was also another plus —her attitude—which constantly kept her in a growing mode. Often it astounded me that as she grew older biologically, emotionally, mentally and spiritually, she continued to stay in the spring of her life—perpetually, as it were, blossoming. She never lost her enthusiasm for learning something new. This one trait, more than any other, seemed to keep her unfadingly, eternally young.

I have to believe that accepting oneself means keeping oneself teachable. Mother kept her mind open to development and exposed it to many varying concepts, philosophies, theologies and ideals. Amazingly, no new idea posed a threat to her, even if it had a strange or unfamiliar thought process or pattern. She just grabbed hold of lessons from each person and from every arena of her life. Her curiosity was insatiable.

I believe that the ability to learn from life—to be teachable, to even enjoy the often strenuous process of growing —has to start with accepting God's analysis of oneself, and then moving on to self-acceptance, humbly and gratefully, before God and before other people. When my mother called herself "a weak unknown handmaiden" she was not

91

putting herself down or using false humility to describe her abilities and gifts. She was genuinely and gratefully describing herself as she knew her talents to be. Yet, at the same time, everything I know and remember about her, and everything I've read in her personal journaling notebooks, tells me that this was a woman who did not suffer from the paralyzing disease of low self-esteem. It was a most awesome experience to be the daughter of a woman who, on one hand, as Paul wrote, had "a sane estimate" of her capabilities; and, on the other hand, whose responses and reactions to people and to life did not come from a lack of self-respect.

I remember once sobbing to my mother about a terribly unpleasant episode. I related that a week ago I'd been called to fill in for the well-known Gospel singer, Tony Fontane. He'd canceled his concert at the last minute due to illness. I'd changed all kinds of plans, dropped everything, driven over two hundred miles, and had gotten there in the nick of time to give an hour-long concert. It wasn't one of my finer musical moments. On a scale of one to ten, it was probably a five or a six. What I really struggled with was the fact that, afterwards, a number of people were so annoyed about Tony's canceling that they came up to me and verbalized and vented their anger. In particular, they detailed their emphatic dissatisfaction with me. (I didn't have to guess that they weren't too keen about my program.) Now, that species of ordeal doesn't make one feel in the least way good about one's talents or gifts; nor does it do a whole lot for a performer's sense of self worth.

"I want to quit singing," I wept to my mother. "I just want to disappear and stop being a 'public person.'" On and on I wailed. My mother's response was great. She took my painful experience and my torn up feelings seriously. She *believed* my pain. Then, reaching down into her own storehouse of wisdom, she came up with a verse in Galatians.

As I look back on it now, it was a pivotal point for me and the flowering of my own self-esteem. I can hear Mother's precise diction as she quoted, "Let every man learn to assess properly the value of his own work, and he can then be glad when he has done something worth doing without depending on the approval of others" (Galatians 6:4 *Phillips*). Another version of that verse ends with, ". . . and won't need to compare himself with someone else" (TLB).

Where did she get her own balanced sense of self-esteem, if it were not from accepting God's viewpoint of her? And accepting it so thoroughly that no matter what *she* thought (or others said), her self-worth was a God-established fact. It followed that the next step was easy. I can still hear her: "See yourself as God sees you, Joyce-Honey, and, being secure in that knowledge, allow yourself to freely move on to accepting the complex but beautiful human being you are." There was no evidence of conceit, or of false humility in her words, but a plea for a balanced concept of my identity and of my worth.

In advocating self-acceptance, my mother wanted to drill into my emotions the priority of first accepting God's forgiveness. Next came forgiving self. And, following that, came accepting my natural self—my shining talents and my areas of not so shining mediocrity, my smarts and my stupidities, my strengths and my weaknesses, even my hazel brown eyes (I always wanted blue) and my fine, limp, unmanageable brown hair (I always wanted blonde). My mother dearly hoped I'd learn these important principles by watching her daily life choices, *not* her pointing finger. So, in watching, I saw all kinds of examples and absorbed many lessons in the process.

I observed that in accepting herself as God saw her, she was then enabled to accept her own *strengths* and to forgive her own *weaknesses*. Most of us pick one or the other to accept. But she had a balanced view of herself. For instance, she gauged her talents accordingly, knowing explicitly where she was talented and where she was not. As I stated before, she had a great love of communicating with words, and she was comfortable with the knowledge that she had the gift of teaching and counseling. However, she freely acknowledged that her very outspoken Hungarian tongue

93

could be, and sometimes was, a major concern that needed not only acceptance but controlling as well. I stood in awe as I watched her blend of acceptance, including both her unique gifts, her idiosyncrasies and her less desirable traits.

I've known women who have never been able to accept their strengths or forgive their weaknesses. I think of the women I know who could never forgive themselves for certain physical attributes such as having very large feet, or, as a friend used to point out, her "ugly hands." People who cannot acknowledge their wonderful God-given talents are then further crippled in their spirit because they find it impossible to forgive themselves of their shortcomings or their weaknesses.

Another example of my mother's balanced self-acceptance was that while she adored music and could play hymns on the piano, she readily accepted the fact that singing was not her gift. Her diary revealed that she dreamed of being able to sing, and she fantasized about how wonderful it would be to play the violin like Mr. C. But with her practical mind she accepted the reality that the gifts of singing or being a violin virtuoso would probably not happen in her lifetime, at least not on this planet.

She once said to a friend of ours, "Any songs I sing now are sung by my Joyce." And although she could play simple music on the piano, when my twenty-years-younger sister, Marilyn Celeste, began sight reading Chopin and polishing off the classics with gusto, my mother simply sat back in her chair and listened to her daughter's fingers fly across the keyboard, playing the songs for her.

Another one of mother's gifts was her incredible ability to take a small can of something, add whatever tidbits were in the refrigerator, and make out of it a mouth-watering, delicious meal. She accepted this gift rather nonchalantly. She also could recycle anything, if necessity demanded it. This, too, she accepted and took in her stride. If she needed furniture, drapes or carpets, she'd take whatever she had on hand or could scrounge or create out of other people's throwaways; and, either by refinishing or re-sewing or

94

re-adjusting—presto! She'd change a castaway into a "please keep me" piece.

However, mother was also accepting of her less than special gifts. For instance, she didn't have the slightest knack or *savoir faire* for arranging hair. Actually, I think it was unfair of her to pass this down to me, as I still don't know what to do with my hair. I'm pleased to report that a few years after she died I had a wonderful dream about her. I saw her in heaven. She was looking vibrantly alive, radiantly healthy. Then I noticed that her hair was beautiful—all soft and curly around her face and looking as if it had just been done. "Well, good," I remarked, "I see they have hairdressers in heaven." She broke into a huge grin, lightly touched a curl by her forehead, and shot back, "They certainly do."

Mother also accepted her seemingly limitless supply of energy and drive. But, here again, she also understood her need for relaxation and for resting. As she became more ill with cancer, she paced herself in ways she'd never done before. For instance, I remember, from my childhood, that she cleaned house at night. That way the phone didn't ring, I wasn't practicing the piano, Dad was not studying or sermonizing in the den; nor did he ask her what was for lunch. At midnight she didn't have to race off to teach a class, go sit quietly with a hurting person, or take care of the myriad of details in her life as a woman, mother, teacher, counselor and pastor's wife. So, she cleaned at night, and into the early hours of the morning. Where she found the energy only heaven knows.

After her mastectomy, we talked about stopping the nocturnal cleaning and vacuuming. She assured me that when she could no longer do it, she'd get someone to "do the floors," as she called it. We both knew that the time would come, but, for then, she cheerily said to me, "Oh, Joyce-Honey, you know that late at night there are no interruptions. It's a wonderful time to clean and vacuum. You should try it. Besides," she added, "it's the very best time to pray!" Since I knew she prayed for her children along with other people and requests, I wasn't about to interfere with

95

her cleaning schedules. Not too long after that conversation, though, she accepted the fact that her strength and energy were ebbing, so she made other arrangements. Quietly, she found a woman in their church to take over for her, and she continued her prayer time during those wee hours of the morning when sleep was impossible. There were no regrets, no griping, nor any stubbornness—just the acceptance of what her life-sapping illness was doing to her.

For all of her life, as I observed her, my mother gave every indication that she accepted herself in totality. She acknowledged and readily used the quality gifts God gave to her. She understood her good, even gifted abilities as well as the weak or unbecoming traits within her. She accepted all, the good, the bad, the wonderful, even down to the least desirable. Again, I'm positive that her self-confidence, her security, and her unflappable composure were largely due to the fact that *she believed God.* She believed he loved her, she believed he saved her, and she believed he forgave her. This was not some theological tenet that she expounded or taught to others. It was her everyday reality. She *chose* to believe God and take his word that she was his child. She acted and responded on her stored belief system. That system did not fail her, even when breast and lung cancer were voraciously eating away the earthly house I loved so much. She accepted her destiny with praise and great dignity.

Watching her trust God's direction, even when it meant she was in the process of accepting the fact that she would be leaving us, was an astounding experience. We watched as she swallowed hard and accepted the reality that she would not be around for my brother's or sister's wedding. I held her the day she realized she would get to know only two of her grandchildren. She grieved that earthly ties were being rudely parted asunder. She assimilated the bittersweet knowledge that life, as she knew it, was being taken from her and coming swiftly to completion. Still she believed God's assessment and evaluation of her soul, as well as his promise of heaven, and, serenely, she gave over to a subtle, yet magnificent acceptance in her final days.

As I remember mother's kind of acceptance, it brings to mind the incredible and rare character of Joseph in the Old Testament. How I loved his steadfast determination to accept all the good and all the sordid circumstances of his childhood. Think of it. He accepted and forgave his ten downright cruel half brothers, as well as his proud and loving father, Jacob. He knew the love of his beautiful mother, Rachel, and his younger brother, Benjamin. Before he was thirty years old he had resigned himself to the horrors of being thrown in a dry well, sold as a slave, taken to Egypt and being put into prison for a rape he did not commit. By the grace of God in whom he trusted, Joseph became the Prime Minister of Egypt. How remarkable! How faithful is our God!

Perhaps as no other biblical character, Joseph led and set the pace for those of us who would believe God, accept his love, his mercy, and his plan for our lives. I feel certain, from reading my mother's notebooks and listening to her Bible study tapes, that she drew enormous wisdom and strength from the story of Joseph's choice to never let go of God's unchanging hand. Perhaps Joseph was her role model; truly he is mine.

Enough reminiscing! Lets open another facet in the gift of acceptance.

After I had thoroughly appraised the gift of accepting God and the gift of self-acceptance, I came to the third and last gift. It was nestled in the bottom of the box just waiting for me. It was, as I'd suspected, the gift of accepting others.

Finally! Here was something I could fully comprehend and appreciate. But, as I lifted it out to take a closer look, it crossed my mind, ever so subtly, that I may not be as smart and savvy as I had imagined. Of course, I now understood the principle that I could never begin to accept others if I had not traveled the road of accepting God and accepting myself. Yet, was it all that simple?

Again, I searched my memories for the clues my mother may have left for me. It occurred to me that, from time to time, I'd wondered how she so rapidly, el pronto, in fact, accepted other people. I could see how she, or anyone for that matter, could easily accept the good and the kind people, the talented and the famous people, the smiling, gurgling, angelic babies, and the gentle old saints of God as they rested and waited for heaven's summons. No trick to this. It's not difficult at all to accept the good and gentle people around us. That's the effortless part of accepting others.

But, I wondered how mother managed, without hesitation or bitterness, to accept the disagreeable and notably mean people, the ever critical and constantly judgmental people, the sergeant-majors in the Christian army whose marksmanship as grenade throwers made them legends in their own time. The acceptance of these complex Christians is hard to understand. Yet my mother showed a surprising willingness to accept them. I knew the names of some of them. These brothers and sisters who had brought about varying levels of pain in the lives of my parents during their thirty-seven years of ministry together. How did Mother accept the hypocritical, the antagonists or even the people who were merely energy drainers in their lives?

I must have assumed that Mother possessed some secret formula for forgiving and accepting others. That somehow she wore a disguise which hid her hurt feelings and damaged emotions. Or maybe she collected the wounds of her heart and placed them in some undisclosed safe deposit box. Perhaps God came to her rescue, in a unique way, and provided a special measure of grace which gave her the miraculous ability to ignore the pain and accept her enemies—even her beloved enemies.

I believe now, in retrospect, that God did her no such favors. The only secret Mother possessed, especially in regard to the people who had wounded her, was her clear understanding that not only had God forgiven her sins and weaknesses, but he had forgiven *others* as well. God had forgiven even those people who were her enemies. He forgave them their sins, their faults, and their weaknesses, just as he had done for her. She began to see others as God saw them: *forgiven.*

I was sixteen when Mother gave me a sterling silver education on accepting people who were everything from merely disagreeable and unfair to those who were downright wrong. And since everyone involved in this incident was a Christian, the lesson made an indelible mark on my memory and in my life.

My father was the dean of men and occasional fill-in professor in what was then a small Bible college. During my parents' first year there, my dad's salary was $150.00 per month plus room and board. We lived in three small rooms at one end of the second floor of the men's dormitory. (Such an education—living in the boys' dorm!)

My mother, long accustomed to accepting God's place for us wherever that might be, coped astonishingly well with the unpredictability of the hallway hazards and the raucous, window-rattling noise levels of living in that dormitory.

She cheerfully endured, without a stove, a washing machine, or even a phone. For our evening meal, she brought food from the college kitchen to our rooms. Lovingly she whispered over it all, added her own magic seasoning touches to the bland, institutional food, and turned it into indescribably delicious feasts.

My brother, Cliff, or "Coke," as he named himself, was an active three-year-old toddler, so Mother had her hands full with "rescuing him" from the students' rooms and losing him occasionally in the dorms or in one of the many classrooms or practice rooms.

How she kept up the pace I can't imagine. Her life and family kept her constantly and fully occupied. Certainly, she didn't need or consider an outside-the-home job. But all it took to change that was one look at the room on campus which the students laughingly referred to as the "library." Being in love with books and a voracious reader, she surveyed the inside of the library and knew she'd found her place of service for the Lord and for the college.

She immediately volunteered to make a real library for the college. Enrolling in night school, she took the necessary courses to become a certified librarian. She set up the cross-filing systems and, for months on end, marked, catalogued and shelved books. Many books had been donated over the years, but most of them were not only without index cards but were still in the boxes they came in. I'd never seen her work so hard and so long. It was an enormous task. Yet she was almost euphoric in the satisfaction of seeing an authentic, bonafide library taking shape under her leadership. The college was grateful, so they gave her some student help and $25.00 a month as a token salary.

Not too many months after she decided to tackle this project and was working night and day in the library, keeping house in the dorm, caring for Dad and our little family and maintaining a ridiculous schedule of all other responsibilities all at the same time—I came home from high school with a request that I knew was doomed to a "No." With a league of unbridled qualms racing through my mind, I somehow found the courage to ask my mother what I could do about going to a movie that the music department was making a requirement for all music students.

I knew that both my parents were obligated to comply with the college administration policy declaring that they and members of their family would not drink alcoholic beverages, would not dance and would not go to the movies. As I recall, there were other issues and rules, but these were the Big Three.

I explained that the movie was the story of the composer George Gershwin. It was entitled *Rhapsody In Blue* and, "Please, could I go?" It was a rather hopeless shot in the dark, but Mother kept her wits about her, didn't panic, and surprised me by calmly saying, "Let me think about it and pray over it."

A day or so later, still calm and quite composed, she said very matter-of-factly, "I'll *take* you to see the movie." It's an understatement to say I was a mite surprised. I was a *lot* surprised. The word astounded comes to mind.

100

Then, not losing her poise for an eye blink, she launched into a run-through on her logical reasoning. She explained that she felt it was important for me to study the music and the lives of musicians from Bach to Gershwin. I suspected that she, like millions of mothers before and after her, had endured and suffered through years of hearing her child pound the piano during practice time. At that very time I was trying to learn "Rhapsody in Blue," and, in general, was destroying it. Perhaps she felt, *Take the girl to the movie, anything to help speed up the learning process.*

At any rate, I recovered from my state of shock and finally managed to ask, *"You're* going to *take me*? But, what about the rule about movies?"

Mother had indeed prayed and thought it all out. She reasoned that because she believed in my musical gifts she did not want me to miss the story. And because she did not know many of the students or teachers and preferred that I not go with strangers, it was settled. We'd go together.

Not too long ago, I saw that same old film on television, and tears rimmed my eyes as I recalled the wonderful time Mother and I had—taking the bus to downtown Pasadena, California, laughing and crying all during the movie, and loving every second of the experience. Even now the memory of her courageously taking me to the film touches me deeply, for I know what the sacrifice of love that night cost her.

About two weeks later, my parents and I were instructed to appear at a special meeting with the college board members and the president. We walked in and sat down around a large conference table in the main board room. I can still see it all in technicolor in my memory. I had no idea why the meeting, or why I'd been asked to come. I took my demeanor from my mother whose head was held up high and who was dressed in her "best outfit."

I listened in stunned silence as each board member sitting around the table, including the president and his wife, asked my parents if it was true that Marion had taken Joyce to a movie. The next question was "Why?" My mother gave them the same answers she'd given me. "I didn't want her to go with strangers or to miss the Gershwin movie." The third question was directed to my father. "Why did you allow them to go?" My dad feigned ignorance and just sort of shrugged his shoulders as if he had not been consulted nor had been a part of the decision. I remember my rising anger towards him as I felt he was letting Mother dangle in the wind.

With awesome swiftness, and no time out for deliberation, the president cleared his throat and handed down their opinions and their punishment. He explained that they would let my father remain as the dean of men provided he would never let such a thing happen again. Then the president looked at me, and his words were not about the movie. He had decided that it was a convenient time to tell me that because some students complained about my practicing the piano in our end-of-the-hall home, I would have to use one of the practice rooms in the basement of the dorm. But, if I did practice in our rooms, I was to confine my playing to a half hour in the morning or an hour, between five and six o'clock in the evening, when the students were at dinner and not studying.

The president's rather mild rebuke to my father, and his instructions to me about piano practice gave me no hint as to what was coming next. It was as if this was *the* moment everyone had been waiting for. The main event. The object of their scorn was seated before them. She had not repented of the sin of going to the theater *and* had compounded her errors by taking her daughter along with her. The stoning began in earnest.

Each person told her how despicable she was as a woman and how she had failed as a mother. Each Christian educator viciously vented what had to be stored up anger from his own life. Even the president's wife expressed shocked outrage that Marion would not only "do such a thing" but that she "showed no remorse." The president closed the meeting by announcing that because Marion Miller had violated the school's ethics and moral codes so flagrantly,

102

she would no longer be qualified to work with the students or be employed as the school's librarian.

Bingo. The last stone hit its mark. Frantically, I looked at my father, urging him to say something in her behalf, to speak up about how unfair it all was. But he sat there staring down at the table. Then, I looked at Mother, and with my eyes told her that if Daddy didn't say something, I was going to! She silenced me with the softest look I'd ever seen, patted my hand and whispered, "It's all right, Joyce-Honey. It's okay."

We were dismissed. I remember leaving the room with more hatred in my heart towards those people around that table than I'd ever experienced before. Good Christian men and women abusing the power they held in their hands, in the name of God.

We went back to our rooms. My dad conveniently disappeared for a few hours. I was angry and paced the floor in the main room. I don't remember where Coke was, but I do recall that my mother sat down at our small dining room table, and stoically folded her hands in her lap with the tears just streaming down her face.

My teen-aged outrage opted for revenge. How I wanted to sue them or take whatever hurtful action we could for their fat sickening smiles and their "thank God, I'm not like you" Pharisaical attitudes. But over and over again that afternoon my mother replayed her position: "God will take care of things . . . God loves me, your father and you children. . . . In God's time, he will make it up to us. God even understands your highly motivated desire to take revenge; but, Joyce-honey, don't you know that vengeance is in God's hands—not ours? God will take care of them and our hurts and broken spirits." Several times she said, "I know it doesn't feel like God is aware of all of this—it feels more like the bad guys are winning—but, Joyce-Honey, God *is* in control. He loves us and we can trust the Lord to take care of us."

I countered angrily, "But, how can you just sit there and take it? Those people sat around that conference table, self-righteous hypocrites . . . acting like your character and integrity was just short of being a fallen woman. They pronounced you a failure as a mother and then they fired you. They are acting as if you're too tainted with sin to be allowed to enter the hallowed halls of their newly established—thanks to you—library. And certainly they made it extremely clear that you're not fit to work beside any student, as if you're a poor specimen of Christian womanhood!" But Mother just sat there, head lowered and shoulders bent over the table.

Today as I read, "The Lord lifts the *fallen* and those *bent* beneath their loads" in Psalms (Psalm 145:14, TLB [italics mine]), I remember how bent and stooped over she looked, sitting at our table, and yet how wise she was in knowing the lifting and the straightening up would come from God.

But, at sixteen, about all I could see was the smug and pious people who, without an ounce of justice, had sought to annihilate my mother. And not for one minute did I understand *or* agree with Mother's attitude nor her willingness to leave the getting-even part to God.

Mother squared her shoulders finally and seemed to pick up after that episode. She went about her life with a graceful spirit and without any apparent traces of bitterness. She even snuck back to the library, that forbidden city of books, late at night, until she finished the last of the cross filing and book markings.

As for me, I remained angry and puzzled by Mother's serenity. She was unshaken in her acceptance of the board members' decisions. What happened over the next six months still boggles my mind. For it seems every time we turned around, either my parents or I, or all of us together, saw each person who had sat around that conference table either coming out of or going into a theater, a movie house, or a bar.

Still, my mother refused to use the information we'd unwittingly discovered, and would say nothing to vindicate herself.

In my immaturity, I was really riled. I'd had it with Mother giving those board members so much grace, especially after we'd found them in such compromising positions and situations. Yet she continued to accept them without so much as a flicker of resentment; nor did she seem to have the slightest whim to expose their transgressions. I watched her responses and told myself that it just wasn't *Hungarian*.

"It's not fair," I reasoned with her. "You have a right to speak up in your own defense . . . . After all, God gave us this golden opportunity to put them on the same hot seats they put us on!. It's time to expose the college's hypocritical and nonsensical rules and disciplinary actions! They are a bunch of Pharisees, whited sepulchers, and we are in the perfect position to take action against them!" I was shouting adamantly. (There's nothing more adamant than a sixteen-year-old who is filled with "righteous" indignation.)

But Mother kept seeing those people through God's eyes . . . as forgiven brothers and sisters in Christ. One day, she looked at me sternly and said, "I will do no such thing . . . and neither will you, Joyce-Honey."

A lot of water has poured over the dam since the night my mother and I saw that movie together. It's also given me a long time to analyze and draw on the lessons of accepting God, myself and others. Aging and living, particularly during the bizarre "unworld" experiences of the last excruciatingly painful five years of my life, have provided me with many occasions to replay my memory's video of my mother's ability to accept the people of God who wounded her so severely.

I know now that, at sixteen, I could only see those people through my own chipped and cracked lenses, but my mother saw them as God saw them. *Forgiven.* They were her forgiven brothers and sisters. As to her part, she made the choice—between taking care of something she felt was critical to my musical development and breaking a rule to which she had previously agreed to abide.

I don't doubt for a moment that her mind recalled Jesus' breaking rules—like feeding his disciples corn and healing the sick on the Sabbath, or talking to the Samaritan woman and intervening at the stoning of another woman. The law was right, but Jesus came to introduce mercy and grace into the law. From her life long studies of the Old and New Testament, Mother knew Jesus' theology was based *not* on temporal rules but on healing relationships.

She recognized that Christ's death on the cross was forged out of his great love for "whosoever." She'd experienced this love and forgiveness of God, by her own choice, and she lived the principle out in daily practice. My dear mother knew that people, even those who misjudged her and disciplined her for breaking the rules, were forgiven also. On that basis, she accepted them without reservations, qualifiers or bitterness. She took John 4:11 seriously. "Beloved, if God so loved us, we ought *also* to love one another."

To my knowledge, none of the sanctimonious people involved in making that decision at the Bible college ever spoke to my parents about it. No one apologized, confronted, defended their position, or even tried to explain their responses or actions. Years later, when we were talking about some of the unfair and unjust incidences and experiences my mother had gone through while in the ministry, we touched on the time she took me to that movie. She laughed, shook her head and said, "I really did do that, didn't I?" Then I asked, "Mother, if you'd known that *Rhapsody in Blue* would cost you your librarian's job, or that the board would be so vicious in attacking your personhood, or that Daddy wouldn't lend you any support—would you still have made the same decision?"

Her smile was as gentle as her answer, "Of course, I would."

"But," I probed, "didn't you want to get back at them just a teeny bit?"

"Nope," she answered quickly. "I felt certain that God would do whatever pleased him about those people. Of

106

course it hurt terribly, but I could relinquish my anger and resentment knowing God loved them too—and, like me, they were his forgiven children.'

The irrefutable lesson that my mother handed down, is this: whether the people who hurt us are our brothers and sisters in Christ or not—Jesus has told us to love and to pray for one another. This includes everyone, even our enemies.

I believe that it was self-evident to Mother that not only was she forgiven and loved by God, but that he had graciously forgiven her beloved enemies for their faults, their shortcomings and their sins. Perhaps she knew, too, that it wasn't up to her to decide who was forgiven and who was not. As she loved the people who were hateful to her, she must have felt that was not enough. She took another step and accepted them under whatever circumstances prevailed, or in whatever condition she found them.

At this moment in my own life, while I am still hearing the indignant, angry voices of Christian leadership, while an occasional speaking engagement is suddenly canceled on the advice of a former friend or associate, and while I'm still labeled by some as "disqualified for God's service," that sterling silver gift of acceptance shines most brightly in the dark and broken places of my heart. It's as if all my devastating experiences have done nothing but polish the silver to a shining luster!

Like my mother, I'm beginning to understand that God has forgiven me, and because of that same amazing grace and unconditional love shown me, he has forgiven my own beloved enemies. The people in Christian leadership whom I feel have hurt or abandoned me are *nevertheless* dear and precious children of God, *just as I am.* I may not want to rush into seeing them as forgiven by God, I may not feel too comfortable in accepting their judgments and criticisms, and I may not be well enough from their woundings to eagerly jump into acceptance; but, in the bright light of honesty and reality, and because of past lessons, I've no other choice. I must lovingly accept others if I am to be a follower of Christ. I'm convinced that the only way to accept others is to constantly remind myself that God has forgiven *them* too!

There is nothing easy or simple about the gift of accepting others—especially those who inflict on us their varying degrees of pain. But I know I have come through the past few years of severe and traumatic wounding, like millions before me, because of God's faithfulness and the remembering of my mother's willingness to see others as God sees them.

What is it we've heard for years from physical fitness experts? "No pain, no gain." I remember well the pain I felt at sixteen, on seeing my mother rejected and ostracized by the college faculty and staff. That experience wrote in wet cement across my rational mind, "Joyce, don't be stupid—it's not worth it to be a Christian. It's ridiculous to invest a dime of your life's resources into *that* kind of hypocrisy."

But God knew the total sum of all the facts about the people and that experience. He knew the pain would teach us life-giving lessons, producing large measures of growth in our lives. He knew the status of forgiveness and the choices which would be made within the hearts and minds of each individual involved—even mine. He knew that, in time, not only would I grow from the experience, but that even the memory of it would be beautiful in a beneficial way. He also knew that Mother would not be around to remind me of his faithfulness or of the great joy and wonder in the gift of accepting others.

So, our loving heavenly father untied the ribbons and peeled off the wrappings from my memories and, while it's not been an effortless exercise, he has led me through the doorways of recall. In doing so, he's eased my pain and comforted me with his peace and hope.

With hindsight I understand that the movie incident, so long ago was like a bushel of seeds planted for future harvesting. While my bones were still knitting together, I could feel the emotions of joyful release and peaceful acceptance, despite the pain of my brokenness. In time, God replaced the bitter bile of inner anger and resentment with the same honey and wine he serves all his children.

Acceptance! No wonder it's an elegant gift, suggesting great wealth. Francis and I are rich beyond measure because some of God's precious children see us through the father's eyes.

Before I go any farther about accepting God, myself and others, there is one more tender but strong and resilient lesson my mother tucked away and left me in regards to this business of accepting others. She took Paul's words, in Ephesians, very much to heart. Paul was dying and in prison, and Mother sensed the importance of what he said, so she listened closely. Paul's message to the Christians who lived in Ephesus was for her quite meaningful in light of her own dying.

I beg you—I, a prisoner here in jail for serving the Lord— to live and act in a way worthy of those who have been chosen for such wonderful blessings as these.
Be humble and gentle. Be patient with each other, making allowance for each other's faults because of your love. Try always to be led along together by the Holy Spirit, and so be at peace with one another (Eph. 4:1-3, TLB)

Mother believed the Bible with her whole heart, but she was absolutely passionate about believing Paul's words on making allowances for people's faults and living at peace with one another. Her list of "faults" encompassed all kinds of people, and dealt with all types of "faults"—from flaws and imperfections to blundering mistakes and bad judgment. It was quite a list. According to her, people's "faults" could be:

their weaker or lesser attributes,
their differences,
their mental, sexual or emotional disorders,
their physical disease or state of contagiousness,
their undesirable or irresponsible traits,
their lack of education and training
their disfigurement or unusual features,
their unsavory past or present,

109

their poor or wrong choices,
their personality, or temperament, or idiosyncracies.

But I think, if I were to put mother's concept about making allowances for the "faults" of others into one brief sentence, I feel she would want me to know that: *I was to accept and make allowances for people's warts and wounds.*

In observing my mother, as she dealt with the complexities of accepting the warts and wounds of others—whether they were physical, mental, emotional, or spiritual wounds, and no matter who was blamed for causing them—it required no great burst of brilliance on my part to see the essential point Mother was driving home. I knew instinctively that the marrow deepest in the bone, in this lesson, was emphatically: *One must make allowances for others' "faults" without belittling or maligning their personhood,*

without devaluing their worth,
without destroying their credibility,
without ridiculing or poking the finger of humor into their
  sorest spots,
without criticizing or judging their choices,
without castigating or chiding them for their size, or their
  fat or lean bodies,
without undermining their hopes and dreams,
without triggering them into despair.

Over and again, she drummed into my head that we were to make allowances for others' faults without maligning their personhood.

Not to mention out-and-out lying, slander or libel, Mother felt that one who merely bad mouthed a human being for his or her particular warts or wounds was definitely displaying and responding with unacceptable behavior for a follower of Christ's teachings. Belittling another person (she was adamant), was *not* what Jesus, the apostle Paul, or the New Testament had in mind.

I was taught that we Christians were to make allowances, to be kind and loving toward one another, and to live at peace with all God's children. That's true acceptance, and that kind of acceptance is as far away from rejection as you can possibly get. I could hear Mother explaining—"Make no mistake about this, Joyce-honey, we are to accept one another, especially people's warts and wounds, with a soft gentle spirit, a warm compassionate heart, and soothing words of grace honed from our own hurts and bitter experiences. And, we are to touch others with healing, not hatred, in our hands."

My mother wanted to show me both sides of the coin on accepting others. While she was very firm on accepting the faults of others, she was equally as firm and committed to accepting a person's strengths, individual specialties, talents and gifts of their personhood. You might think the process of accepting one's obviously good traits wouldn't require an educational session. After all, what's so hard about accepting good, even great things about another human being? Good point. But Mother knew about the hidden pitfalls here—so she cautioned me, "When we accept people for their strengths, gifts, skills and talents, we must do so *without jealousy or envy.*

From my own background and perspective, let me walk you through one type of God's "gifting" . . . and, through my eyes, let you see what it's like to have a dramatic-type gift or ability. Clump together in your mind, the people you see performing on some stage or platform, the people of the arts . . . the musicians, actors, actresses, artists, preachers and priests, even writers, to name a few. To me they are the "spotlight" performers with highly visible and recognizable talents and gifts.

On February 5, 1932, her mother's birthday, Mother recorded her disappointment in her diary that her baby had not arrived. She knew, without the benefit of sonar or amniocentesis, I'd be a girl, so she named me Joyce and wrote of her unqualified belief that I would be "a sweet singer of songs for God." I was born the next day.

By the time I was three my Mother taught me some two hundred or more choruses and children's songs. By the age of four, I was regularly singing in my father's Sunday morning and evening church services. During the week my play house was the empty church sanctuary, just as it was for many preacher's kids. I played make-believe church endlessly. Growing up I heard my mother tell me each day—in one way or another—that I was special. Later she referred to me as "a child set apart." From the beginning, though, I was always performing. I *loved* it and found it came as easily and naturally as breathing.

Before I was ten, piano, elocution and voice lessons were a part of my life. Once I caught on to the basics, practicing for hours every day was included as a normal part of my growing up process. My earliest memories are those of performing, usually at church, but many times in our living room. For this and many other things I'm deeply grateful for my parents—Mother, in particular—because of her patience and persistence in coaxing me into developing and polishing the natural gifts within me.

Later as I began to perform publicly in school, church and civic programs, I became acutely aware of the reactions of other people towards me and to my performances as a "spotlight" talent. Many beautiful and thoughtful souls took the time to wholeheartedly cheer and urge me on in my music. I'll always remember how nurturing that felt . . . it made the long hours on the piano bench and all those boring vocal scales much more bearable. But I began to notice that sometimes after a person saw or heard me perform, their attitude toward me changed. Sometimes my peers backed away or grew cold toward me; while others just sort of dropped out of my life. Quickly I found out that a musician, like an athlete in training for the Olympics, has a limited and sharply curtailed social life. Partying, keeping the welcome mat out all the time, going places, having fun with friends and generally maintaining social relationships with people were difficult at best.

Even at church where I thought I'd find the most acceptance over my "spotlight" gifts, I was constantly bumping into this remark, "Joyce, you're so talented it makes me sick." It was mildly humorous the first few years, but later I thought that if I heard that line once more I'd be sick. I could not imagine the appropriate response to people who made such comments. And most certainly, I didn't have any idea of what to say to the countless stream of women who, apparently struggling with low self-esteem, cried, "How come God gave you all that talent and he didn't give me any?"

Mother always gave these people unlimited grace and felt that for reasons known only to them, or perhaps only to God, they were unable to accept the performing gifts of others. She also felt that when a person responded to me in that way, I was not to take their statements to heart nor as a valid critique of my work. I was, however, beginning to experience the scary truth of Proverbs 27:4. "Jealousy is more dangerous and cruel than anger." Mother advised, "Don't be hard on them, Joyce-Honey. Perhaps they can't forgive you for your gifts. Or, maybe they are unaware that God has given everyone—*including them*—their own unique talents. They can't see their own strengths and gifts, so they find it difficult to accept the talents of others."

To follow up on those thoughts, my dear mother did something she was good at. She wrote out a scriptural guideline for my acceptance of others—regardless of their talents, their qualifications or their status:

> Love each other with brotherly affection and take delight in honoring each other (Romans 12:10, TLB).

At that point in my life, this scripture—especially the part about honoring each other—brought about a change of attitude. It worked wonders in my ability to accept others. I applied these lessons first to pastors and then to "spotlight" talented people. By accepting my own gifts (or lack of), and then the gifts of others, it then becomes possible to move ourselves to honor others' abilities. It was a very freeing experience.

Performing publicly in any arena is a highly competitive thing. Egos are fragile; stress factors run well up and over the crack-up, burnout levels; and the competition is fierce. So, to accept others in your field *without* resentment or jealousy is to dump excess baggage off the back of your emotions. It feels light and enables one to give his or her full attention to the creative work God's gifts demand.

However, lest I sound like I am some great paragon of virtue who wipes jealousy and resentment out of my mind as soon as I see it raising its little green head, and that I always and instantly accept others en masse . . . . nooooo, not so! Just because I've been accepting the "spotlight" people for many years, and it appears that it comes reasonably easy to me, I must tell you, once in a while the undesirable trait of jealousy pops into play when I least expect it—and far too often. Difficult as it is to admit, the fact is: *Some* people really are easier to accept and honor than others. Once in a while I'm forced to deal with my inner struggle over jealousy and resentment. I'm hesitant to embrace acceptance and take delight in someone's gifts. I should know better. Wonder why I do that?

The Bible tells us to rejoice with those who rejoice and weep with those who weep (Romans 12:15). Most of the time, I think it's far easier to weep with somebody than it is to rejoice and be happy with them. Many of us have no problem or trouble at all weeping and comforting our friend who filed for Chapter 11 and then slid into bankruptcy. Anyone can befriend the hurt or brokenhearted, but it's another ball game if we are called upon to join the celebration and rejoice with a friend whose grandfather or uncle left him $100,000. Why is it, when we hear of a friend's good fortune, that our resentment, jealousy—even a tad of bitterness—eats its way through us, leaving a trail of sourness in our system; and "being happy" for them, much less rejoicing, becomes an unnatural response? I think it takes a very special person to be delighted when success or good fortune comes to another.

This is not a test, but I wonder . . . do you have as much trouble as I do in accepting and honoring *some* people? For instance, how do you respond to accepting and honoring

114

the people you rub shoulders with every day, the people you're related to, or maybe those down-home folks you've known all along? How do you accept the people in the following scenarios?

The woman next door who cooks infinitely better than you?

The man at work who drives an expensive new car, yet you make the same salary?

The teenage daughter of a friend who makes head cheerleader, while yours doesn't?

The brother-in-law who calls you and is so thrilled about his large Christmas bonus?

The friend who has far less training, skills or experience; yet, she gets the job for which you both interviewed?

The lady in choir who sings the solo almost every Sunday, and you're asked once every seven years?

The college aged friend whose wealthy family pays for everything, while your son goes to school and moonlights two jobs?

The friend whose son goes to Harvard while your pride and joy drops out of college and joins the army?

The woman whose house is already crammed with furniture, who wins a washer and dryer from the local appliance store?

The military buddy who gets a promotion the same day you're passed over?

The friend who goes in for a face lift and eye tuck and comes out looking ten years younger than you?

The neighbor who ran against you in the local school board election and won?

I strongly suspect that we all know a few reasons why it is difficult to get *beyond* resentments and jealousy with regards to the "good turn of events" of our family, friends and neighbors. It certainly is *not* that we don't want them to

115

come into good happenings, or to receive God-sent blessings, or to have promising doors open . . . it's just that we look at others' fortuitous circumstances through our own disappointed and sometimes prejudiced eyes. Our vision is clouded by our own pressing problems, discouraging failures, energy sapping fatigue and sad regrets of our own lost chances.

We respond to others out of our own needs and well-defined deficiencies. I doubt that we are really aware that the jealousy and resentment we feel toward others may not even be a conscious decision on our part . . . but actually is an involuntary response, a knee-jerk reaction, right out of our subconscious level—based not on another person's circumstances, but our own.

Somehow, when I take this all into account and remember that my ability to accept others starts with my acceptance of me first, and that my own circumstances may dreadfully hamper my efforts to accept and know others—I am reminded of a lady in a red dress.

As I've mentioned before, I've sung and spoken, since covered wagon days, for Mother and Daughter Banquets. On one such occasion, I arrived at the church, for *once* in my life a bit early. I found the gymnasium all set up with tables to serve dinner and to present a program for several hundred mothers and daughters.

The decorating committee had definitely met, and they had done a wonderful job of transforming the cavernous gymnasium into an elegant lattice-lined indoor garden setting. I could smell the delicious aroma of food floating out from the adjacent kitchen. But not a living soul was around. I wondered how I was going to let the chairman know her banquet soloist and speaker had arrived. I stood on one foot for awhile, checked my letter from the church secretary to be sure I had the right date, time and place, and then shifted to the other foot. I felt a casual sense of foreboding. About then, however, halfway down the right side of the gym, a woman in a bright red dress came bursting through the double doors. Hurriedly she threaded her way through the maze of tables towards the kitchen on the opposite side. When she was almost in the middle of the gym, I called out, "Excuse me . . . ." The woman didn't stop or even slow down—she just kept rushing toward her designated target.

Again, I called, "Excuse me. Can you tell me who the chairman is for tonight?" She glanced over her shoulder at me, just as she was about to hit the kitchen doors and said, "Sorry, I'm busy. Can't talk now. Be back later!" And she disappeared into the kitchen.

Ooooohhhh-kay........

I put my record albums, my "brains" folder containing my speech notes, and my purse down on a chair by the main entrance. Maybe if I just stood there looking like a lost, hungry puppy some kind soul would take me in and feed me. After what felt like a long time, but really wasn't, a woman walked in from the parking lot, her arms loaded down with papers, a folding card table and some other paraphernalia. Glad to see her, I wagged my tail, happily barked, "Hello there!" and rushed to aid her. But, she barely raised her head and mumbled something, possibly it was "Hello," and proceeded to set up what was to be the ticket table. I stood there forlornly, not even slightly engrossed in watching her line up the reservation sheets, tickets, name tags and cash box in their proper little order. Would she never finish? Just as I was about to ask her where I'd find the chairman, the lady in the red dress came out of nowhere again.

I waited until the two ended their chat, and then I touched the right sleeve of the red dress.

"Excuse me, but I really do need to speak to the chairman . . . ."

The lady whirled around, met my eyes, stared at me for a fraction of a second, and then shouted, *"Do you have a ticket?"*

Startled I began to stutter, "Well, ah, no—because you see, ah, I'm the . . . ." (Speakers never have invitations or tickets. We have been signed up by phone or by mail, or both, for months. We are just to *be* there.) Instantly I knew I was the straw that broke this lady's back, because her face

117

matched her dress, and she berated me with a scorching red hot lecture on how disgusting it was for people to just show up at the door without reservations or tickets!

On and on she ranted, informing me that a sign-up sheet had been in the lobby of the church for three Sundays in a row, that one announcement after another had been made in regards to the importance of having reservations etc., etc. Somewhere in this exchange, after I'd tried a second time to explain why I didn't have a ticket, she threw up her hands and shrieked at me, "I can't believe it! It's unbelievable! People won't sign up for reservations. They just *show up*. They just walk in the door expecting to have a place. I can't do that." She was pointing frantically at the tables. "I have 253 dinners and places set for tonight, and I don't have room for one more person."

I made one more valiant attempt to tell her why I was there without a ticket, but she shook her head "no." As she stormed away from me she said, "I can't deal with you! I just don't know how I'm supposed to put on a dinner when people just show up at the door!"

I admit that I was enamored with the idea of doing her great bodily harm. It was frustrating. I stood there realizing my kids were junior higher's, and if I'd wanted to be roasted for dinner I could have stayed home.

By now mothers, daughters, and grandmothers were starting to pour into the gym. They were all enthusiastically talking to each other and busily getting their tickets and name tags. I tried to get one of them to nod at me or to respond to my "hello," but it didn't work. After I'd said "good evening" to a number of women who without exception gave me a hasty brush off, I seriously and, yes, rather fondly considered going home.

Now I'm not saying that there in that gym I heard the audible voice of God—but, I'll tell you, as I began picking up my things and had happy thoughts about getting out of there, I definitely heard *someone* say, "Don't leave. I've an important lesson for you to learn."

So I went back to my "helloing" and giving all to making contact as the women came in. After another fifteen minutes of forcing "hello's" on the women, I knew there was no way I was going to get these mothers or even their tiniest daughters to speak to me, so I gave up. Actually, I'd been through this type of scenario (of women not responding to me at the door) but I admit that this time my feelings were a tad hurt.

Hurt feelings, however, turned out to be a lesser problem because at that moment boredom set in. A word or two about boredom. It's not a good thing when a creative person gets bored. Creative people tend to overcompensate for the problem and invent games to take up the slack. My game, I decided, was to pretend that I was the official church hostess for the evening. I wished I was wearing one of those giant hostess buttons, but, as you know, no ticket— no name tag even, much less imaginary button!

I positioned myself in the middle of the main doors so the women couldn't miss me. They'd be my captive audience as they waited in line for their tickets and seat assignments. I was so taken with the idea of playing hostess that as effusively as I could gush I welcomed and hugged all the startled faces of the mothers, daughters, grandmothers, friends or neighbors as they came in. I was not only enthusiastic and gracious, I was loud. Soon I could hear the women forming little groups behind me asking, "Who *is* that woman?" I was blissfully delighted as I heard them questioning my identity. Whether I was Delores, whoever that was, or maybe Delores' sister!

After giving my rousing welcome speech to about a hundred women as they came in, I became bored again and decided to revise my act. So instead of merely saying, "Welcome tonight to our Mother-Daughter Banquet . . . is that your little girl? Oh, my what a darling dress . . . Okay, now, just stay in line here and get your tickets . . ." I added, "And, by the way, you are just gonna love our main speaker. Talent just pours out of her! She's fabulous! She'll be singing tonight, speaking, tap dancing and doing handstands! She's terrific . . . we had to sign her up two years ago (a small lie) just to get her here for tonight . . ." etc., etc.

I had no shame. I loved playing hostess, telling the women all that nonsense. As it was I had a better time and more fun doing that than I had while I was standing around on one foot waiting for a moment to talk to Mrs. Red Dress.

Unfortunately, I ran out of work as everybody was finally seated for the banquet—that is, everyone but me. I took my rose colored jacket and black patent handbag off the chair by the door and sat down on a seat by the back wall. I'd probably still be sitting there except for a darling elderly lady seated at the end of the nearest table. She looked over at me, quickly got up and said, "My dear, you don't have a place . . . . You just come right over here and take my chair!" (I wondered which door she came in and how I'd missed her.) She continued, "Now I'm going to go to the kitchen and get some silverware for myself, and we'll pull up another chair . . . and I want you to meet Mrs. Brown, her daughter Sue, Mrs. Smith, etc. . . . ." She introduced each person around the table, and when she got back around to me she asked, "And dear, what is your name?"

I said, "Joyce."

She smiled, said something about that's lovely and then it hit her. She whispered into my ear, "Joyce who?" I told her, and quickly she responded with, "Oh, my dear, you're our main speaker tonight!" She pointed to the head table and added, "You're supposed to be up there. Now you wait right here. I'll go get our pastor's wife. She's the chairman for tonight." And off she went.

Ah ha! That's right. You got it!

I saw the red dress get up from the head table and start toward me. And, as I watched her, I tried calculating where, exactly, she would be when she'd see me and remember our conversations. I figured it would be about seven or eight feet in front of me, and I was only an inch or two off.

She stopped dead in her tracks. I could see her mental wheels turning and reconstructing our encounters. Her

120

deathly white face started to crumble into tiny broken doll pieces. I have no idea what she said to herself, but whatever it was, it reassured her, for suddenly she regained her composure, straightened up her back, adjusted her panty girdle and confidently strode over to me.

I'm not sure if this was a God-thought or a Joyce-thought, but I distinctly remember hearing in my mind, "Listen up. This is gonna be good." I also had the feeling it would be funny and yet sad. I sure got that right.

With all the diplomacy of a *charge d'affaires* officer, Mrs. Red Dress just waved away and resolved our small, silly little conflict by saying to me, *Oh, if I'd known who you were, I would have asked you in.*

For a second or two I stood there, dumbfounded. All the way over to my place at the head table I kept hearing her phrase . . ." *If I'd only known who you were* . . . ?" I don't remember anything about dinner or whether I kept my campaign promises about the program and lived up to my advanced billing. I kept wondering why knowing *who* I was should have made a difference. I asked myself, on the drive home, why did she have to know who I was before she could let me in or tell me hello or even say "Hi" for that matter?

Why indeed? Why do I have to know your name, your marriage ties, your occupation or profession, your educational training or degrees, your parents, your family's pedigree, your economic status? Why do I have to know the "Who" of you before I ask you in? Before I say "hello." Before I speak to you? Before I'm nice to you? Before I let you sit down? Before I listen to you, or before I give you a cup of cold water in Christ's name?

The unforgettable line, "If I'd known *who* you were . . ." has followed me ever since that long ago night. If I'd left the banquet after my first tangle with The Lady in the Red Dress, as I almost did, I'd have missed this priceless lesson on accepting others.

I'm confident that lady didn't intentionally set out to reject me earlier, especially when I first called to her in that empty·gym. In fact, the first words she said to the audience

121

when she opened the banquet were, "I hope you all know we are a *friendly* church, and we're so glad you're here."

Her problem undoubtedly related to herself, to her fears, her insecurities, her anxieties, and her stress levels. And if the answer to being able to accept and honor others lies in accepting oneself first—the lady in the red dress probably struggled that night as the pastor's wife and the chairperson with accepting her own personhood. It was almost as if she *had* to know *who* I was, to give me an identity, before she could relate or respond to me.

I wish I could have told her that night that I understood her struggle—but I didn't. I think now she might have been a very fine even caring woman, but one who was under a great deal of stress, and who didn't handle it very well. She also may have been a woman questioning the "Who" of her own identity. We can accept others without knowing "Who" they are, but only after we've discovered "Who" *we* are.

So, dear person, yes, you—whatever your name. You *do* have an identity and you are known, well-known, to God. Please hear my heart on this. It is a wonderful thing to understand that God accepts all our attributes, our strengths, our gifts and yes even our warts and wounds. For he does, he really does. But acceptance is not just some nice little abstract platitude that I was taught by a wonderful mother . . . acceptance is a *God* idea. Acceptance works on all levels. God's acceptance, our own acceptance of ourselves, and our acceptance of others. It's a marvelous healing gift, an incredible legacy to spend and to enjoy.

It may be hard for you to hear my words about acceptance, but, believe me, I know what I'm talking about. Down through the years, especially the recent ones, I knew God not only accepted me but gave me the courage and strength to accept myself. Over and over again in the past few years, he has led me to new and unfamiliar doorways. And the godly people behind those doors opened them wide, pulled me in and embraced me. They never asked my name, or showed the slightest interest in the significance of the who, what, when or how of my life. They just knew a human being when they saw one, and they didn't stand around wondering what they should say to me, or deciding whether I could "up" their social status. Those beautiful God-sent people ushered me in without a ticket, seated me without question, and served without hesitation a banquet of love, respect and acceptance in God's name.

Since God did that for me—and it still stuns me with joy —I know this is possible in your life, also. In fact, it may just be true that the bigger the heartache we have, the more the Lord pours out the grace of *his* acceptance on our brokenness. And isn't it just like him to give us other people? Not people who are poverty stricken—but people who are wealthy beyond belief in the elegant gift of acceptance, and who take us into their hearts in spite of not knowing who we are or what we've been through!

Chapter 5

Very late the memorable night of November 12, 1966, I told my dad I'd finished packing away "Mother's things," pointed out which box went where, hugged him goodnight and left Reseda for the long drive home.

The solitude of the quiet, almost empty, freeway provided me with a collecting space for my scattered thoughts and served me well. There was only an ounce or two of energy and strength left inside me as I went back over the traumatic events of the day. The persistent grieving process had exhausted and pushed me past the shock stage on into the awful reality that Mother was not away at a hospital, taking an extended vacation, or back in Michigan caring for some family member . . . she was gone.

This stark fact pounded like a drum beat in my head. I would never on this earth pick up a ringing phone and hear her chirpy voice ask, "Good morning, Joyce-Honey. What wonderful thing has God done in your life today?" I knew, too, as her "sweet singer of songs," I wouldn't be able to repeat David's words to her: "I will sing unto the Lord for he hath dealt bountifully with me." And I also knew that I wouldn't hear her usual come back, "Bountifully, how?"

My memories were poignantly beautiful, but before I'd driven a few more miles I'd realized something else. For, while it was true I wouldn't be seeing Mother in person or hearing her over a phone, God had done a lovely thing tonight as I'd boxed up her things. As I was packing her things I'd actually entertained the fear that three cardboard boxes were all that was left of her. Instead, the Lord had opened up the vaults of treasure and let me have a peek at her "things" that were mine forever.

In case she was listening, I said aloud, "Mother, guess what? After I'd packed your clothes and cleaned out the den closet, the Lord spoke to my heart and mind about some of the gifts you left me. Namely, my inheritance. It was the emotional equivalent of being summoned to an attorney's office to hear the reading of Marion Uzon Miller's will—and finding out that you had left me a wonderful and totally unexpected fortune."

As I drove toward my home in Pomona, I reviewed the gift of humor and smiled—remembering the way she used to put runs into her nylons as she got out of a car—and the look on her face when she'd say, "See how they're wearing them these days." I told Mother that God had described the estate she left me as a "warehouse packed full of treasures."

I suspected the years would reveal other gifts, but for now it was enough for me to know about two or three of them. In my heart of hearts I knew that no matter how many gifts she'd left me, I was really going to lean on this inheritance. Little did I know that twenty years later I'd still be leaning!

In the spring of 1967 I wrote about the experience of packing away Mother's things for my editorial page, "Over a Cup of Coffee," in *King's Business* magazine. Space was limited, so I selected only a few gifts for the article. After the piece was published in the magazine, I put aside the idea of writing about the other gifts or even the "mother's things" experience itself. I didn't completely forget my wonderful legacy—I just laid it temporarily on a back shelf in my mind.

Then, my first book, *Let's Have a Banquet—or Will $1.36 Be Enough?*, was published in 1968, and one book after another followed. Rearing two teenagers, keeping a family and home running smoothly, continuing a daily radio program, and speaking and singing at churches all over the country crowded out my thoughts about being the beneficiary of a fortune. However, I couldn't forget about those incredible gifts, even during that busy time of my life. No, to the contrary, I opened them and used them regularly. And when I look back on it now, I thank and praise God for his exquisite, just-right timing. He would always present me with another gift for my mind and heart, just in the nick of time, for my need or my encouragement.

The years and the books have rolled on, and now more than twenty years and twenty books later, I've discovered I'm the recipient of many more gifts. During the span of time since the night of boxing up "Mother's things," I've inherited among others: the gift of wonder, the gift of relinquishment, the gift of choosing, the gift of caring, and the ebullient gift of serving. Those heaven-sent presents need to be verbalized and I intend to do that when the time is right.

Then, in 1985—the year I experienced divorce, most of my speaking engagements were cancelled for the next three years; so it came as quite a surprise and honor to be invited to speak on Mother's Day in both Sunday morning services for a church in the Northwest. I'd done more than my share of Mother and Daughter banquets, but I had never been invited to give a Mother's Day message in any church. As hurt and terribly depressed as I was by all that was transpiring at that time, I was nevertheless pleased by this new request. Quickly I accepted their invitation.

However, once I'd agreed to go and the date drew near, I had more than my usual stage fright tremors, and the misgivings within me were legion—about my sanity and my wisdom in accepting such an engagement. My state of mind concerning the major problems in my life caused my thoughts to fragment into a million pieces. My emotions were dangerously fragile and quite unstable.

I must be out of my mind! How could I have accepted this engagement? Why had I thought I'd be whole enough to give a message to anybody—at anytime—much less now on Mother's Day? But, by April of that year, it was too late to cancel out; so, in the cold sweat of panic, I frantically got out my old "brains" folders from past Mother and Daughter Banquets and started searching for something, anything that would point me toward a thirty-minute Mother's Day talk. It didn't work. My search was a futile waste of time.

Then, as I was reading the *Los Angeles Times* newspaper, I found that its pages were filled with pre-Mother's Day advertising. There were gifts both large or small, but all seemed to be guaranteed to assuage your guilt over mother. Some were pure fantasy land gifts. Very expensive. Others were cute. Little knickknacks and cards. As I read the copy on many of the ads, they made me smile with their brand of pop psychology. So I thought, "Well, at least I can start my message on a humorous note by reading these ads on Mothers Day."

Some of the advertising copy read like this one from I. Magnin's exclusive Beverly Hills store—

How extravagant of you! To give Godiva chocolates on Mother's Day. She'll say you shouldn't have. But you'll be glad you did. Only $10.00 a 1/2 lb.

Ah, yes, *only* $10.00. For *half a pound*???

The Broadway department store had a whole series of pictures of Mother's Day merchandise, and above each item they ran a heading:

"Because mother is business minded . . ."
(Pastel colored calculator)
"Because mother just got her ears pierced . . ."
(Earrings)
"Because mother is a gracious hostess . . ."
(Glasses and carafe set)
"Because mother goes for casual clothes . . ."
(Designer skirts and blouses)
"Because mother is always one jump ahead . . ."
(Dress shoes and tennies)

But May Company won the Madison Avenue advertising prize. They ran a single line across a full page of the newspaper, which simply read, "I love you Mom and I didn't forget Mother's Day is May 10th."

127

It was as I was still chuckling over the ads and planning how to use them as an opener for Sunday's Mother's Day service that it suddenly hit me!

What in the world was wrong with me? It was stupid to worry about trying to come up with suitable material for my talk. For, even in my shattered condition, I knew all I had to do was to share a few of the gifts of the inheritance Mother had left me.

Quickly I dug out the old copy of my *King's Business* article, written in 1967; and, greatly relieved, I went to work framing out the points of my message. I chose the gifts I wanted to share, and listed four of them from my stockpile of treasures.

Then an inner voice questioned, "Why not end your talk on Mother's Day with this gift?"

"What gift?" I couldn't see it anywhere in my mind's eye.

"This one . . . the gift of faith."

Of course! I must have been blind. The gift of faith was a natural for Mother to leave me. Wonder why I didn't discover it before? Actually, as I think about it, my mother's faith had been one of the brightest burning lights about her.

By faith Marion asked Christ into her heart. By faith she accepted God's forgiveness and her salvation. By faith she was a courageous woman who did not merely mouth the words, "I believe God"—she went out every day of her life and *acted* on that belief. By faith she took God at his word, trusted in him and then she responded and acted according to that faith. In the process, her accomplishments were gloriously splendid.

She understood that a life of faith is not one of sitting around waiting for all systems to be "go" before getting up and doing something. Nor is it a life of faith when you hold back until you're sure that everything will have the traditional "they lived happily ever after" ending. She knew that faith ventures boldly outside into the troubled chaos of life *before* one knows the outcome and before one sees efforts crowned with success. A faith that doesn't act and move on its belief is not faith. It is merely a shadow of what it could be. Mother chose to act by faith *before* she saw the results. The Bible says that faith without works is dead, and Mother got that right—early in life.

Time and again, even from the decision she made to take me to see the Gershwin movie, Mother—not recklessly, but wisely and cautiously, went against some very popular opinions, breaking an established rule here and there, but bravely *in faith* doing what she felt before God she should do. As in the decision about the movie, she "acted" before she knew how it would all turn out, before she knew she'd be shunned and humiliated, before she knew that in the end she'd lose her librarian's job. In faith she presented the problem to the Lord in prayer, weighed the factors involved, and came to her final decision very carefully. She chose to do what she felt God would have her do and to leave the outcome, positive or negative, in God's hands.

Yes! Definitely my Mother's Day message, in 1985, would be about the gifts of my inheritance, ending with the splendid and glorious gift of faith.

Off I went to the Northwest and on Sunday, Mother's Day, with all the mothers in the audience holding fresh carnations, I delivered my "Inheritance" talk for the first time. It went a little better than I had expected—considering the fact that I was drowning in the flood waters of mental and emotional pain.

One heart-tickling thing was that I didn't have to begin my message with the light touch from the *Los Angeles Times* ads. The pastor did it for me. It was wonderful! The hymn he chose for the congregation to sing before I spoke that Mother's Day was, "Faith of Our Fathers." It struck my funny bone, and nothing could have stopped me from verbally tap dancing around that idea for a minute or two. But, come to think of it, that was in 1985—the first, last, and only time I was ever invited to give a Mother's Day sermon. Which probably serves me right.

But now, five years later, I'm writing out that very same talk, and pouring the gifts from my inheritance into this manuscript. I've had no trouble at the beginning of each chapter describing the way those gifts are packaged and how they look in my mind's eye. The gift of humor's wrapping paper was old and dog-eared. Honesty's gift was wrapped in vibrant Hungarian colors. And, of course, the gift of acceptance was sheathed in gold foil and silver ribbon.

A few nights ago, as Francis was returning home from our publishing offices, he came through the door with his usual greeting of, "What do you have to read to me?" And, untypically for me, I floundered about, explaining in the vaguest terms why I'd been unable to write more pages on this gift of faith. We had a lengthy discussion as I tried to decode my problem. I described how each time I'd begun a previous chapter I'd instantly been able to visualize the gift package. In my head I'd seen the wrappings, ribbons, even the bows of every gift. They had all promptly materialized in my mind. But not so with this one. The gift of faith was different.

"Why is that?" I asked Francis. And then we both looked at each other and almost said simultaneously, "Of course! You can't see faith! Nobody can!"

We were both hearing the litany of our childhoods. Our preacher fathers had quoted and taught the verse, "For we walk by faith, not by sight" (2 Cor. 5:7, KJV). And, all our lives we'd heard the other verse, "Now faith is the substance of things hoped for, the evidence of things not seen" (Heb. 11:1, KJV).

And how could we not recall the wonderful paraphrase buried deeply in our hearts of that very same verse?

What is faith? It is the confident assurance that something we want is going to happen. It is the certainty that what we hope for is waiting for us, even though we cannot see it up ahead. (Heb. 11:1, TLB).

No wonder I couldn't describe the package. The gift of faith comes in a transparent box. We can't see it's top, sides or bottom. We can't define it's perimeters. In fact, sometimes it seems not to be here even when it is. The gift of faith, like oxygen, is real—but you can't see it or grab it. Skeptics tend to think faith is not a basic, essential need; that we can jolly well get along without faith, and that its relatively unimportant to life here on this planet. But acting as if faith, or oxygen for that matter, is unimportant because we can't see it or hold it in our hands only reveals the limitations of our minds. Faith is as essential to our spiritual lives as oxygen is to the physical.

Dr. Phillips Brooks, the great theologian, wrote,

> God is not a crutch coming in to help your lameness, unnecessary to you if you have all your strength.
> He is the breath in your lungs. The stronger you are, the more thoroughly you are yourself, the more you need of it.

Ah, there it is, think of it, *faith is our spiritual oxygen.* It not only keeps us alive in God, but enables us to grow stronger. And we always need more of it.

Besides being invisible, faith is characterized by paradoxes. Such as this one: *Faith is a gift from God that we can't earn with good works. But at the same time, if we don't practice good works our faith is dead.* That's wild! I don't even have an illustration or comparison to explain this paradox. In fact, part of what is so unexplainable about faith is that *we can't conjure up or manufacture faith on our own; yet faith is the necessary ingredient for our coming to God for salvation:*

> For by grace are ye saved through faith: and that not of yourselves: it is the gift of God: not of works, lest any man boast (Eph. 2:8,9, KJV).

I can't go to a neighborhood market and buy a pound of faith like a pound of ground coffee. But, somehow, God continually urges me to keep on believing. He nudges me to pray, to persevere, to move on and to make choices—thereby exercising my faith. He encourages me to freely ask for his help and his direction. In doing so, I realize that to *ask* and then to *act* is living by faith. God seems to honor those who continually exercise their faith.

And talk about paradoxes, just ask yourself, when do we *desperately* need faith? When do we wish we had a measure of faith more than at any other time?

Certainly not when our job and finances are going great guns!

Not when our pain is over and healing has come!

Not when our relationships with others are simply, as the British say, just smashing!

Not when explanations, meaning and understanding come easily!

Not when our questions have been answered and our doubts have vanished!

Not when our fear, stress and anxiety levels are at an all time low!

And, absolutely, *not* when the fishin' is easy!

We need faith at precisely the time when there's unequivocally no rhyme, no reason and no solutions left. No way to turn. No where to run. We never need our faith in the Lord more, than when there is absolutely, humanly speaking, no way out. When all roads seem to lead into dead ends or box canyons. When nothing *whatsoever* makes any sense. When people and problems are hopelessly scrambled together and we fear for our sanity.

This is when we are to accept God's gift of faith! Preposterous? Perhaps. But over the years of watching my mother, Marion Uzon Miller, I saw episode after episode in which God gave her a powerful faith at the exact moment when her life was utterly chaotic and when the circumstances she faced were mostly no-win situations. God seemed to make the gift of faith available when the trials in the fiery furnace burned at the highest temperatures, when there was no human or natural answer and when everything else was stripped away.

It seems to me that the quintessential core of having faith is believing an unseen God and trusting God's invisible love and power. However, what makes this so difficult, to the human mind, is human emotions. When I go through an incredibly horrible ordeal, I lose a dearest loved one, or I face seemingly endless series of broken relationships and difficult hardships, my emotions become crushed, discouraged or depressed beyond the point of hope.

I want desperately to fix the blame on something or someone in order to ease my pain. And sometimes I'm not sure who exactly wronged me; other times, I think I know *who* only because it "appears" that way. Then sometimes I feel that the tragedy I am experiencing has happened because somehow God is to blame. Or, at a minimum, he is neglecting or ignoring me, so it feels as if he doesn't care about me. Sadly enough, my emotions become my worst enemy at this moment because emotions can't tell the difference between what is real and what appears to be real.

This is when faith, my belief in God, must keep an attitude of love and trust. By faith, I must do as my mother before me did. I must believe, without immediate evidence, that it is not God's nature or heart's intent to pull away from me. In short, I must give God grace. "Forgive" him, if you will; and trust him as I've never trusted before.

Now, before you get upset with my suggesting that I, or anyone, needs forgiveness in our heart toward God, let me hasten to explain. When I talk of "forgiving God," I'm not suggesting that God has wronged me and therefore needs *my* forgiveness. I mean rather that when a person, in reality, harms me, and when it only "appears" that a person harms me, in both cases, my emotions react the same way. Therefore, to have these feelings of doubt and distrust towards God because of my dire circumstances is not in any way abnormal. But to hang on to them and to nourish them

133

prevents me from moving on to wholeness and healing with God.

It's nice to know that my negative emotions are not a surprise to God. In fact, my state of mind or behavior during a time of crisis is hardly news to him. He's had a lot of experience and history with his children and their inability to distinguish the difference between what's real and what we perceive to be real—especially when it comes to our view of him.

Check out the story of the prophet Elijah. It's recorded in the book of First Kings, He had the most incredible, wonder-working, miracle-making adventure of his whole career as a prophet, winning an awesome victory over four hundred and fifty of Baal's prophets? Of course he did. What a prophet! What a man of faith! But, in less time than it takes to write this down, Elijah hears that Queen Jezebel has put out a contract on his life and is threatening to kill him within twenty-four hours. The man not only freaks out in fear but catches a bad case of amnesia. Elijah forgets all that God has just done through him, and his emotions take a long walk on a short Judean cliff. Which is to say, this great man of faith is reduced to a frightened shadow of his former self and, scared out of his wits, he runs for his life—literally a distance of about eighty miles. He winds up alone, even without his servant, with no shelter in the middle of the wilderness. Devastated and close to physical and emotional collapse, Elijah, the *great* prophet's prophet, cries out to the Lord, "I've had enough!" Incorrectly he concludes that God is finished with him, so he cries, "Take away my life, I've got to die sometime and it might as well be now" (1 Kings 19:4, TLB).

Bless his darling old heart. Can't you hear him? To Elijah it *appeared* that the same God who had given him one incredible victory after another, and had done many astounding feats and miraculous healings, was unable to save him from the wrath of one wicked Queen Jezebel.

The truth was Elijah, one of the greatest men of faith of all times, was a mere mortal. As do we other mortals,

Elijah *felt* and *rationalized* that God had abandoned him, leaving him no option but escape through death. To his mind and shattered emotions there was nothing left to do but die.

Actually Elijah's emotions were giving him a *very* distorted picture of God. It was as difficult for the prophet as it is for us today to keep an attitude of love and trust towards God when our view of him is colored by "appearances." In reality and hindsight from the scriptures, we know that God gave Elijah a refreshing sleep to refuel his depleted, exhausted body and emotions. There were even ministering angels sent by God to care for his needs. But that's not the way Elijah saw it!

We are blessed that God doesn't judge us or deal with us according to the downswings of our moods, our overactive and destructive imaginations, or our emotions which have run amok. We must, therefore, remember the past goodness and mercy of God. We need to, in faith—blindly as it were —set aside our "feelings" and give him grace, show him a "forgiving attitude," and keep putting our trust in his great integrity. And we need to remember this particularly when we feel estranged from him, regardless of what things *appear* to be. When we are able to recall the intent of God's heart, and set aside our distorted emotional perceptions, we can find the bridge back to him, and our relationship with our heavenly father is miraculously restored. I think Catherine Marshall summed it up beautifully when she wrote,

> Then came this revelation: When life hands us situations we cannot understand, we have two choices. We can wallow in misery, separated from God. Or we can tell Him, "I need You and Your presence in my life more than I need understanding. I choose you, Lord. I trust You to give me understanding and an answer to my 'Whys?'-only if and when you choose."

(*Light in My Darkest Night*, Leonard LeSourd, Publ: Chosen Books, 1989)

When I was very small, my father wrote a little chorus. He sang it for me, and later, with me, for all the time he was alive. It was about faith, and one of his unpretentious lines ran, *"I know the Lord will make a way for me."* Both he and my mother had believed solely by faith that God would unquestionably make a way for them.

Mother's notebooks and letters kept an exceptionally good record of her courageous journey of faith. On the last Christmas Mother was alive, my brother was in the navy and about to go to Vietnam as a marine corpsman. Mother was valiantly waging a war against the cancer within her, but she had no idea who was winning or that she was in the final months of her life. Still her faith was at once vibrant, yet peaceful, and glowing. In a letter to my brother, dated December 13, 1965, she wrote,

> My dear Cliff,
>
> I was so disappointed to hear you cannot be sure of coming home for Christmas, while you are so near us before going abroad.
>
> I am enclosing the $20.00 I want you to have, now that you bought the watch, do with it as you see fit.
>
> My prayers will go with you wherever you go. Be courageous and trust God to help you at all times.
>
> Marilyn has done a great job of wrapping the Christmas presents and the den just oozes with Christmas.
>
> At this Christmas season, I thank God for the joy and peace I have in my heart—made possible by Him.
>
> Tomorrow I go to UCLA Medical Center, for about three or four days, for injections of 5 F.U. Fluorouracil. I am in God's care, and I know whatever comes of it [chemotherapy] I am not afraid. Thank God that Christ is with me.
>
> My son, God has a chartered course for us all. He whispered so sweetly to me last January that if I put Him first in my life—He'll see that I come in second.

So, I put myself in His care, and ask Him to pilot the course laid out for me and for my dear family.

God bless you, Son. You will face hard, trying days—but, I know you'll come through with flying colors.

"Be not afraid, neither be dismayed for the Lord God is with you wherever you go."

> Lovingly,
>
> Mother

Often I have thought about her words to Cliff, "God has chartered a course for us all," and her line which followed: "So, I put myself in His care, and ask Him to pilot the course laid out for me and my dear family."

When do we need faith? Not when things are all right but when they are all wrong. I suspect that one of the songs Mother loved the most was the one about trusting God, the pilot. And whenever she asked me to sing it for her, she would say, "Now, Joyce-Honey, sing it slowly . . . I want to hear and take in every word."

Sometimes when my faith would falter,
And no sunlight I can see,
I just lift my eyes to Jesus,
And I whisper, "Pilot me."

Chorus:

Fear thou not, for I'll be with thee;
I will still thy Pilot be,
Never mind the tossing billows,
Take my hand and trust in Me."

> ("I Will Pilot Thee," by Mrs. Emily D. Wilson, public domain, Pub. 1927)

Faith is trusting God as the unbelievable, unreal and unthinkable events happen to us. Faith is trusting God during the pain of our greatest hurts. Faith is trusting God to pilot the course he has laid out before us. Faith is placing ourselves in God's safekeeping. Mother had faith, but certainly she had no guarantee that asking God to pilot her course, or putting herself in his care, would assure the exact results *she* wanted or imagined. Being human, she desired clear sailing and an easy voyage free from sea sickness and violent wind storms. Nevertheless, by faith, she chose to trust the pilot.

The Christmas of 1965 and the early months of 1966 brought incredible testing of her faith. Still she trusted God and his ways, though the events of her life seemed to have lumbered over her like a slow moving cement truck, crushing the life out of her.

If she questioned or doubted God's chartered course, it didn't show. She trusted him steadfastly and encouraged us, family and friends to do the same.

Early in the last January of her life, Peter Uzon, her father, suddenly died. The snapshots taken the day of his funeral show my mother in a somber black dress with a hat to match, looking like a tired old lady twice her age. Still she trusted God. I watched her as she fought her chemotherapy nausea and as she grieved for her father; yet, she kept on trusting and believing God.

In one of her notebooks, written shortly before this time she must have been struck by this verse in Philippians.

Let this mind be in you, which was also in Christ Jesus (Phil. 2:5, KJV).

She had put at the top of the page, "The Mind of Christ," and then wrote,

What an amazing transformation could be seen in my life if I accepted God's constant offer to let His love direct my spirit (attitudes and mind) and let "this mind be in you . . ."

Imagine the joy of being able to think His thoughts and reveal His love to others?

138

In the midst of all the physical and emotional pain she endured, Mother was able to keep her faith, believing God without losing her sanity because she allowed "God's mind" to direct her spirit and attitudes. "Let this mind be in you" was no religious platitude to her, but the mighty hand which held her's when she was fighting cancer and dealing with the death of her father.

Suddenly, in the midst of all this grief, everything drastically changed. Mother went from dying—on Christmas Day, with her skin ashen gray—to springing into rosy radiance by her birthday, the fifth of February. God graciously allowed the chemotherapy to work, and pressed the gift of five gloriously healthy months into her eager hands. The remission was about as dramatic as it could possibly be.

Mother fairly glistened with new, radiant health. In the halls of UCLA Medical Center, everyone who knew Mrs. Miller-Honey, as they called her, excitedly discussed her awe-inspiring turn around, her marvelous progress and the striking effectiveness the 5FU treatments had on her.

However, on the fourth of July, while I was in the middle of celebrating at a family reunion picnic at my parents' house, I kept looking at my mother and wondering why she had chosen to wear an old, rather beat-up looking sleeveless dress. Then, I saw the swelling in her upper arms and knew they were too swollen to fit into any of her dresses with sleeves. Slowly something very close to an arctic freeze began spreading over my heart that hot July day.

I guessed the fluid was building up from the lungs, causing the swelling as it had done before, and it seemed dreadfully clear to me that God had not cured her, but had given her a five-month remission from the agony. The murderous cancer, welcome as the Medieval black plague, was back.

A few days later, remembering the shabby sleeveless dress she'd worn on July the fourth, it occurred to me since the swelling was back in her arms she probably didn't have any dressy clothes she could comfortably wear to church. So, I went to the fabric store, bought some pretty silk material in soft shades of pastel pinks, lavenders and greens, sewed together a sleeveless shift, as they called them, and took it over to her.

It was then the last week of July. I knew, with a sinking sense of grief, that things were rapidly going, as doctors say privately to each other, "sour." Mother's voice sounded weak and tired, and her pain virtually resonated and oozed through the phone receiver. When I asked how she was feeling, she played no games, but leveled with me, explaining that the fluids and swelling were causing heavy pain. She had already called her doctors and reported that they had advised her to come to the hospital ". . . if not today, tomorrow."

Near the end of our conversation, as she was walking me through some other dreadful side effects of her illness, her faith came through like a pinpoint of light from a beacon a great distance away. It was obvious to me that she was still, even *this* hour, trusting God to pilot her course. I felt certain that her faith had never been stronger, though the cancer had never been so victorious. She confided, "You might say, this is a very bad day, physically, but . . ." here she paused, and then the tone of her voice lifted buoyantly, "spiritually and mentally, I couldn't be better!"

The next day, in her home in Reseda, just an hour or so before my dad drove her to UCLA Medical Center, naturally my mother took the time to write me a long letter. I say *naturally* because it *was* natural. It never mattered where she was going, even if it was only overnight, mother expressed her love by phone or letter. She simply did not go out of town, on a vacation, to a church conference, a retreat, or to the hospital without writing a "love letter."

The practice of and dedication to writing letters like that started with her when I was a little girl in Owen Sound, Ontario, Canada.

One morning, a woman, a member of Dad's congregation, was killed by a car moments after she had walked her twelve-year-old daughter, Alice, down the street to school. Earlier they had a typical argument over the girl's choice of dress. When they had reached the corner—the point where the mother was to go one way to work and the daughter the opposite way to school—things between them were so strained and tense that they parted without either saying their usual goodbye or giving each other their warm hugs as they had always done.

Seconds later, Alice turned around to look back, only to see her mother struck and killed by an oncoming car. By lunch time that day, my father had brought the grief-stricken daughter to our home. I'll never forget the scene when I came into our living room. Alice was sitting on the couch crying softly and saying, "I didn't say goodbye . . . I didn't kiss her . . . I didn't wave . . . I didn't say anything . . . ." Looking back on it now, as an adult, I think the unspoken cries of that heartbroken young girl had much to do with her regrets about the unfinished business between herself and her mother. We all think, or try to think, we will live forever. We take life and the living of it for granted. We assume that we will have plenty of time tomorrow, or in future tomorrows, to settle things. We'll have another opportunity to say "I love you," to apologize, or even to hug someone goodbye or hello again.

For my mother, the lesson of that day in Canada left an indelible impression on her heart. From then on, whenever we'd leave each other, never mind how brief or how long a time, Mother made sure she phoned or wrote her children. She always wanted to wrap up any old unfinished business and, more especially, she wanted to leave us with the certain *knowing* that she loved us. She did this *just in case*, and *just on the chance* that maybe something would prevent her from coming back and seeing us again.

I used to tease her a bit over this because I got the feeling that even when I took out the garbage I'd get a letter before I went outside and get kissed and hugged after I came back in. But, even if I did kid her, those letters, hugs and kisses were, and still are, precious and dear to me.

And so, *naturally* in the moments before Mother went to the hospital, she wrote out the feelings of her heart. It was to be my last letter from her. She died seven weeks later. That same letter is before me now—dated July 26, 1966 —and typically, she starts out her message as she started almost every other card, letter or note. She began with her gratitude.

My dear Joyce,

Thank God for such a dear daughter and for her love and concerns for her mother. I especially am pleased with the shift you gave me, and want again, to thank you for it. I wore it Sunday and received many compliments, I might add.

Your radio program was very good today, and I'm sure, helpful to many. I think I'd like to ask you to write it for your page in the *King's Business* magazine. It deserves repeating, for our problem today is Rebellion! Thank God there is a remedy, and that is Christ alone.

For someone who did not have any formal (or informal) training in journalism, Mother most certainly had a flair for it. Starting letters with gratitude for the one you are writing is nothing short of brilliant—and most definitely tends to get one's attention. Then to follow gratitude by declaring your interest in one's work or the strengths of their personhood and directing encouragement their way is the hallmark of a magnificent balcony person.

It touches me deeply that when she wrote this letter and mentioned my writing, I was still two years away from penning my first book manuscript for Zondervan Publishing Company. *Before* I even wrote books, she believed I would!

But her words in this letter were another example of the way she acted and moved in faith. Even though she was fatally ill with cancer, and about to return to the hospital for the painful procedure of fluid draining, she chose to take the time to communicate her thoughts about the "need" for me to write out a magazine article from my radio program.

142

I knew of the consistency of her prayer life, so I was sure she had already prayed, asking the Lord to bless my writing and to touch those who would read it. Then, her body in great distress, still believing God and trusting him, Mother *acted* on that faith, assuring me once more and for the last time in writing, that *she loved me.*

The next paragraph in her letter changed subjects and was full of concerns and personal sadness for her brother, my Uncle Pete, and his family. Mother had learned that my aunt's long-time illness was deteriorating her mind and body; and, now, what little health she had left was slowly disappearing. For Peter, his wife's condition appeared to be a hopeless situation, and Mother had spent much time in prayer on their behalf. This paragraph voiced her loving concern about them and was one of the most lengthy in the letter.

She then commented that she'd received no mail from my brother Cliff, in Vietnam, and enclosed a page from a missionary magazine. It was an article about some dedicated people who were missionaries to Vietnam. I had to smile, because it was she who introduced me to the magic of words and the world of printed pages and books; and here, even though it was a busy morning, filled with arrangements and scheduling, she took the time to include some *printed* material in her letter.

At the bottom of the first page—after her other concerns were expressed and taken care of—Mother finally got down to writing of her own depressing circumstances. It was like her to verbalize her feelings about God's ability to heal his children. And, yes, being the Bible study teacher she was, she dealt with those issues in her most favorite way: biblically. She did not ignore or minimize her problems—her swollen arms and chest, along with other signs, had alerted her to the precarious position she was in—but, with her faith providing hope and her unwavering belief in God, she most certainly wasn't about to discount God's ability to give her the miracle she prayed for and knew her condition warranted. She wrote,

*Today I go to UCLA. I'm sure of the promise and love of God
and know He will completely heal me. He said it was finished
[John 19:30] and by His stripes I am healed [Isaiah 53:5]. He
promises 70 years and by reason of strength 80 years [Psalm
90:10]. I think that a Christian who has the life of Christ [2
Tim. 1:1] within Him can claim health.*

*I do not ask in my merits—but as a child of God, redeemed
[Eph. 2:8-9], I ask in Jesus' name! God does not heal because I
deserve it—but because Jesus paid for it and redeemed me.
Praise God.*

Then, quite abruptly, as if the issue of her healing had
grown too heavy for her to carry one more step, Mother
dropped it and changed the subject. She wrote a sentence or
two about a contact I'd had from a Christian television program that was just beginning in San Diego, and a line about
my Laurie being at camp and her hopes that it would go well
for her. Finally Mother ended this trio of short paragraphs
with a practical housekeeping detail. She wanted to put my
concerns to rest, so she told me about the three women who
were coming the following week to clean house for her.

She then wrote her final paragraph—and the brief lines
take on life right now, fresh as the day I first read them. Of
course I'd read the passage before, many times, but the
passing of time, the place where I now stand, the losses and
the gains of the past twenty-plus years since she wrote this
letter . . . these have all changed my perspective, and my
understanding. I read with wonder Mother's last words, in
the light of my recent "unworld" experiences; and, to my
mind, her words here are of great significance. They are
words she did not want me to miss. She told me of a change
in their weather, and commented,

It's cooler now and so much more comfortable. I think we
should get a cooler for the house, and then I thought of the
expenses. But I opened up a book and read that if you have
a need—go ahead, believe God, and with each step of faith
the financial means will be provided. You know, faith must

144

act—for faith without works is dead . . . and, without faith it is impossible to *please* God. For they that come to Him must *believe* that *He is* a rewarder of them that diligently seek Him.

It's almost noon. I must close and get ready to go at 1:00 pm. So, much love and prayers to you all—my dear children.

And then it looked, to me, as if she stopped writing and contemplated a moment or two about the content of her final message. What did she want to say? What was in her mind? What would be of utmost importance that she'd want to leave as a lasting impression with me? I suspect there were a few moments of deliberation and questions which ran through her mind, because at the bottom of Mother's letter there was a line all by itself, set apart, as if she wanted to emphasize its significance. In her clear, yet exquisitely florid hand, she wrote,

Keep Faith with God—Regardless and Always.

And signed underneath—

Lovingly, your Mother
Also, one of your most ardent fans!

Mom

It was not surprising, and not one bit out of character that in her final letter Mother would leave me a pronounced, unmistakable statement about faith. She'd lived her whole life believing and acting on her faith. Faith was the oxygen to her spiritual lungs. Yet even the ordinary, the mundane decisions such as purchasing an air cooler were brought to God and put through the sieve of her faith. Entirely in keeping with her rigorous yet practical way of working with Christ, she chose to end the letter with her distinct counsel and clear admonishment for me to keep faith with God—regardless and always. She even capitalized the word *Faith*. When I first received and read

145

Mother's letter, in 1966, I was unable to absorb the immense truth and value it contained. I'm sure many of you, when in the midst of carrying out the painful routines of caring for the dying and the needs of your immediate family as well, know what I mean. Somehow we manage to endure; yet, to be able to hear the message of a dying loved one, or to be in a learning mode at that precise time, is very difficult, if not impossible.

A few weeks after Mother's funeral, I retrieved her letter and re-read the last line, *Keep Faith with God—Regardless and Always*, but the same inability to see or hear what she was saying happened again.

I know now that my whole system was still in a state of shock. The term "shell shocked"—which originated in World War II, describing the emotional state of a soldier suffering from combat fatigue—is quite appropriate for what any of us go through during the months following our loss. We are exhausted by the arduously long traumatic crisis preceding the death; and then, after the funeral, we have to deal with others who unwittingly prod us into "normal activities" and who do not understand that our strength and energy have gone . . . evaporated. So we find ourselves pushed into the never-never land of shock. It's no wonder we can't concentrate and find it hard to hear what is being said. It seems to me that sometimes, no matter how powerful or true the words of a comforter are, or even how perfect and well-suited they are for us, we are unable to hear them.

Again, I put her farewell letter away.

Six or seven years later, as I was writing the book *Mourning Song*, I assembled all of Mother's notebooks and letters to use as research material, and, of course, I re-read that final letter. But it's real significance—while I deeply treasured the letter—was still lost on me. At that time, I was no longer in the fresh throes of the grieving process, and had long emerged from the shock, denial, anger and bargaining stages of the newly bereaved; but, again, I routinely and rather quickly glossed over those final statements on faith and took them somewhat for granted. It was an easy thing to do. I long ago accepted my mother as a woman of faith. I knew that . . . well, actually, we all knew it.

It was easy to visualize her being dressed in her splendid garments of faith, looking like a regal statue erected in the middle of the town's square. The statue erected as a monument to her and her faith was there for me to drive by and admire, but I confess I'm not sure I readily saw it as an education for learning about faith. So, in *Mourning Song*, I duly described my mother, the lovely statue of faith, including the "regardless and always" line. Then in 1973, after I'd finished writing that book concerning death and dying I again packed away mother's notebooks and letters, and her closing line on faith stayed tucked away in the boxes with my research materials and papers.

Mother's letter, with its simple but supremely important message, might have lain dormant, neatly packed away in my garage for some future generation to stumble upon— except for the events which shattered my world in 1984.

That year was nothing less than cataclysmic, and it brought with it an avalanche of radical changes. In one fell swoop, the drastic life-threatening ordeals of that year changed the entire course of my life. The world, as I knew it, no longer existed and for a long time I felt as if I was tumbling and falling through a dark void space somewhere between earth and the other galaxies. During that time I spent the hours of the day between being filled with fear, afraid of everything and never knowing from one second to the next who or what would come careening out of the blackness, hitting and smashing into me. Nor did I know whether I'd stay out there, falling through space a year or two, or if I'd stay out there indefinitely. I could feel myself reaching out, grabbing for any straw in the wind to hold to, trying to find something solid to land on. I screamed for God to give me a small something that would break or interrupt the falling process.

Then faith, only a microscopic amount, mind you, gathered itself into a trembling, quivering tiny bird and began winging its way toward me. Faintly at first, then stronger,

147

without actually *seeing it*, I somehow sensed that it was coming out of the vast darkness of nowhere. And above the eerie howlings of the rushing winds, I began to hear the sound of the fluttering wings of hope and faith's voice singing my name. Calling, "Joyce, Joyce . . ." then repeating over and over again, "I'll carry you safely through! Remember! Keep faith with God—regardless and always."

How do I know this? Believe me. I know. I can tell you, dear friend who may be falling like a rock through a dark void this minute, I know that when we are free falling in the nighttime of space, that is exactly when we are most likely to *see* . . . to experience God's gift of faith. Tiny as it may be, appearing as a small speck on our horizon, we feel faith as it comes closer out of the nothingness around us. Suddenly, miraculously, faith is swooping us up, carrying us away through the blackness of night towards the safety of sunlight. Faith's wings are amazingly resilient and powerful, and faith's determination to carry us *all the way* is unrelenting.

It is faith that reminds us that *nothing* separates us from the love of God. It is faith that constantly whispers, "God can be trusted. Don't fret. God will not reject or abandon you." And, in my case, it was faith that waited until the year of my greatest need to dig out my mother's letter and *show* me what she really said. Isn't it strange that often we don't really see or appreciate the subtle manner and ways the Lord chooses to touch our hearts or speak to us —until we are faced with a time when we are most desperate? It's almost as if we come into a delayed inheritance. But it's worth the wait, for God's timing is, after all, exquisite. There have not been too many days or nights, in the last four or five years of my life, that in some way Mother's counsel,

Keep faith with God - regardless and always

has not jolted my thoughts with its electrifying all pervading truth. Yoked to the very core of my being is Mother's word *regardless*.

She used *regardless* as an adverb . . . meaning, I was never, never to give up on God. I was to hang on to him, keeping faith with him *regardless,*

in any case,
at all times,
in any event,
anyhow,
anyway,
in spite of the fact that,
not withstanding,
nevertheless,
none the less, and
no matter what.

This was to be the ambiance of true faith. I was to continue, persevere, endure, and keep going on. I was to do this regardless

of how lonely the night,
of how searing the pain,
of how unfair the trial,
of how cruel the relationship,
of how shattered the love,
of how wrong the choice,
of how broken the dream,
of how sick the abuse,
of how numerous the enemy,
of how strong the guilt,
of how heinous the sin,
of how deep the shame,
of how painful the course of events,
of how unjust the verdict,
of how long the sentence.

Regardless. I was to keep faith with God. It's for sure, God keeps faith with us. Did she know—that discerning, sensitive mother of mine—that God would keep her faith alive in me by that one line in her last letter? Did she have any idea that during my years of great victories and raging battles, holy or sinful choices, successes or failures, I would hear that reminder of hers and reach into my storehouse of gifts and lay hold of this one, the gift of faith, regardless of any and all circumstances? Did she have a divine premonition that twenty-or-so years from the afternoon she wrote those words, I would face and deal with the most difficult times and choices of my life? I think so. She was a woman of discernment. A woman who listened to God through the ears of her faith. I'm sure she was counting on faith's carrying me through the valley of the shadow of death, regardless of how terrifying it might become. More than anything, she wanted to pass down the heritage of faith to me. She knew I'd need it to survive.

She understood perfectly well that faith doesn't forgive our sins and save us. But faith is the shinning angel of light who takes our hand and our will and leads us to the foot of the cross of Christ. And there, because of God's grace and by his forgiveness, we see and find the Savior and our salvation; we are supernaturally and miraculously born into the family of God. However, once we are believers, I don't care what you've heard, faith can't and doesn't solve all our problems. Faith can't and doesn't erase all our tragedies. Faith can't and doesn't remove all the boulders or roadblocks in our pathway. Faith can't and doesn't answer all our questions or supply us with all the meaningful explanations.

Faith simply does what it does best. *Faith leads us to Christ and carries us through.* Faith can and does hold us together when our life is imploding and we feel fragmented and formless. Faith can and does speak to the very center of our viscera, the very core of our essence, and to the very most ravaged remnant of our emotions. It is faith that whispers, "Hang on—God's here . . . Don't give up. . . . It's winter now, but spring soon will come." It is also faith that says, "I may not be able to answer your questions or heal your most grievous wounds, but I'll not leave you. I'm staying with you. I'll take you through this horrible time. I'll

150

carry you over raging flood waters. I'll carry you over the rugged mountains. I'll carry you over the fiery desserts. Hold on to me, regardless.

Regardless.

Don't be concerned or worried that your faith is so small. My husband, Francis, once said,

> Faith, like life itself, is a process that develops from experience to experience, from crisis to crisis, day to day, and year to year. It is something that begins small and *grows through the moments*, the days and the years of our lives.
>
> *(Monday Through Saturday,*
> Balcony Publishing, Austin, TX 1985)

Our faith is a growing thing. I am reminded of a line about faith by Dr. Phillips Brooks,

> You can keep a faith only as you can keep a plant, by rooting it into your life and making it grow there.
>
> *(Perennials,* Dutton, N.Y., 1909)

Mother was not a master gardener. Nor was she some kind of great spiritual horticulturist saint. She simply planted faith in me. She did so without knowing whether the fragile roots would take hold in the soil. She risked planting faith in me, and she must have wondered whether the plant would be well-watered or given enough sunlight. She planted faith in her children with a cautious eye on the weather vane, concerned about the possibility of future storms, droughts, hail or high winds.

She planted faith in me with more than a suspicion that she might not be around to see what she'd planted bursting with blossoms or grown into a mature and healthy plant. But she planted anyway.

She risked whether her children would accept or reject God; and she understood, from the very beginning, that planting faith, programming it into her children's lives, and

151

living out her own faith would not be all that would be needed. But she planted anyway.

She knew that faith, after all, is a gift from God. So faith, like any gift, has to be accepted to be really ours. Faith has to be received by us before we can claim it. Mother, as gifted as she was, could not make the decision for my siblings, or me. She could not choose God for me. She could not accept the gift of faith, in her name, for us. She could only plant faith in the soil of my soul. After that, it was up to God and me.

So it was, after planting faith, Mother stepped back, allowing *me* to make my own decisions.

The integrity of this kind of spiritual character was carefully penned in her diary. On one page marked by the date of 1929 at the top, she wrote,

Spin cheerfully,
Not tearfully,
Spin carefully,
Spin prayerfully,

But leave the thread to God.

After she planted the seed, she daily lived a whole lifetime of faith as an example for us children. Only then was she at peace about doing the most difficult thing of all for a parent—relinquishing her children into God's safe keeping. Mother called it letting go and leaving the thread with God.

Which all brings me to her unique usage of the second word in her last letter dealing with ". . . regardless and always." The word *always*.

I'm certain Mother wanted us as her children (me, in particular) to grasp the sum and substance of keeping faith with God—not only regardless of what happens but for as long as one faint pulse beat is left! In other words, *Always*.

Everyday, at all times,
On every occasion, without exception,
Day in and day out,
Invariably, inevitably,

152

Unfailingly, unceasingly,
Perpetually, endlessly,
Forever and ever, eternally.

When I mentally replay memory videos of the legacy left by my mother, and combine them with my own years of circumstances and hindsight, I can easily visualize what she had in mind concerning the word *always*. She fervently desired that her children would keep on always believing in God. And for me, because I was a grown woman with my own family, I knew she wanted me to keep on always trusting and never give up on my calling. I was to keep faith with God *always*. I can almost hear the sound of her voice, *"Joyce-Honey, remember faith is here, it's God's gift to you. Keep it growing . . . always!"*

The word *growing* is a verb. Mother wanted me to understand that faith should not be held down or imprisoned in static stationary confinement. Faith should be nourished and fed by action. It should be moving out, expanding and increasing. "Verbs," as one long-ago English teacher put it, *"are to do words"* . . . and the verb *growing* is one of the very best.

As I've thought about the idea of planting faith and about the growing of that faith, I suspect that while faith is planted in the garden of our souls, some of us may not receive enough cultivation and fertilization to grow. Some of us may not be watered or given enough sunshine at the very time when the roots of our faith are barely alive and struggling to take hold. In other cases, some of us may be starting to grow, with the buds on our young stems about to burst open, when someone puts a foot squarely on top us, bruising and breaking the plant we are trying to become.

You may not have had a planter of faith such as my mother, but God, our kind, loving creator, is the original gardener of faith. Maybe only he knows who, in your whole existence, was the planter of those tender roots of faith in your soul—before you even knew it was spring and the planting season had begun. And it occurs to me that

153

possibly the people who stepped on you inadvertently or purposely crushed the fragile plant of faith in your life were the very people used by God to strengthen and straighten your tender broken stems. Perhaps *because* of them, and in spite of them, the long process of healing has taken place, and you've become remarkably strong and bursting with blossoms.

As my mother's daughter, I could gauge pretty accurately how life's circumstances would diminish or add to her faith . . . but it didn't dawn on me, until near the end of her life, that I didn't know much about the person who initially planted the roots of faith in *her* soul. Once I asked her if she could remember when it was that she first heard about Jesus. I knew she had come to this country at the age of ten, and that a year or two after being here my mother and her parents became Christians, but I was curious about Mother's very first exposure to the Lord.

She had clear recall of the moment, and in words very similar to these she said,

> I first heard about Jesus when I was walking home from school with the rest of the kids.
>
> There was a lady who lived in a little house on the corner at the end of our street. Every afternoon, just as we'd be going by, she'd open her front door, go in and play the piano and sing songs for us.
>
> For a while, we'd just stand around outside listening. But one day the lady came out on the porch and invited all of us in. So we went, and she taught us all to sing some catchy songs about God and Jesus. She was wonderful to us and we really liked her. Come to think of it, it was in her house that I first heard the song "Jesus Loves Me This I Know."

A nameless neighborhood lady saw the potential and possibility of the "gardens" out there on her sidewalk, and she (God, please hug her for me!) planted the roots of faith into the children who passed by on their way home from school, including one little girl named Marion.

154

Who planted faith in you? Do you know, besides God, who nourished it? I certainly don't . . . but, just think. God had planned for you and for those young slender stems of faith to be placed in you (and in me)! He even planned who and what would "allow" your faith to grow.

It is God who sets the climate for growing faith. It is God who waters, nourishes, even prunes us, and it is God our loving creator who works through people in developing and cultivating our faith.

We really do grow and expand in faith the longer we give ourselves to trusting God. We grow in faith the longer we watch the results of his mysterious ways. We grow in faith the longer we accept the fact that God deals with us, knowing what is actually best for us, and by trusting and believing that God really does work things out for *good* in our lives.

Romans 8:28, that oft quoted verse, begs us to keep our faith alive when we realize its truth. It shouts at us to view our bad experiences as well as our great and glorious experiences as from the Lord. All things working together *for our good.* The scripture asks us to see the long run, the overall plan, and the purpose in God's allowing us to grow.

And we know that all that happens to us is working for our good if we love God and are fitting into His plans (Romans 8:28, TLB).

The people, events and experiences that please or pleasure us most . . . and the people, events, and experiences that hurt us most—*both* are sent or allowed by God. And, from first hand evidence, I can tell you, by faith we can trust the intent of God's heart and believe he has planned good things for his children. And of course real faith is believing God's heart while we cannot see our path, it's direction, the final destination or *any* good coming out of our life's journey.

I can also hear my mother's voice urging me not to overlook another important aspect about keeping faith always.

She prods me into taking action again when she leans over heaven's balustrade and calls down, *"Joyce-Honey, exercise your faith or it will atrophy, shrivel up and become useless . . ."*

Oh, yes. *Exercise*, another verb like *growing*. Now its *"exercise"*—and I have another reminder that "faith without works is dead."

It's dawned upon me afresh that my favorite chapter in Hebrews—Hebrews 11—is filled with one example after another about people of faith, and it is of particular interest to me that the writer has used verbs to describe the particular *action, work*, or *exercise* those people chose to do by faith. They are not only portrayed as *having* faith but as *acting* and doing something based on their faith as well. No, their faith was not a dead, useless appendage to their souls; nor was it merely decoration or window dressings. It was as if they tried, regardless of what was happening to them in their world, to honestly and regularly exercise their faith. Look at the verbs connected with these names. Here's a list of a few people mentioned in this one chapter of Hebrews.

Abel *brought* a better sacrifice . . .
Enoch *pleased* God . . .
Noah *constructed* an ark . . .
Abraham *obeyed* the summons . . .
Sarah *gave* birth . . .
Isaac *gave* his blessing . . .
Jochebed *hid* her son Moses from the Pharaoh . . .
Moses *chose* to suffer with his people . . .
Moses *led* the exodus from Egypt . . .
Moses *kept* the first passover . . .
The Israelites *walked* through the Red Sea . . .
Joshua and his men *walked* around Jericho's walls . . .
Rahab *received* and *welcomed* the Israelite spies . . .

It seems to me that these, and many more, real live men and women of faith—in the Bible and down through the centuries—gave a great deal of their energy and effort to spiritually "pumping iron." Those heroic people seemed

156

to be always, at least most always—at the primary, gut level of life—developing, stretching, and strengthening the muscles and the biceps of their faith.

In the eleventh chapter of Hebrews, the writer records some of the extraordinary deeds done by people of faith. But later, in the same chapter, come the chilling words: "But others trusted God and were beaten to death, preferring to die rather than turn from God . . ." (Heb. 11:35, TLB).

Apparently there were many men and women who exercised their faith with all their might and soul *without* seeing the final results. To my mind, these "others" were the real super heroes of the faith. How they speak to my heart today, in our society and culture whose morning prayer is, "God give me instant rewards, instant gratification and instant everything. Now." The people of faith, in the Bible, seemed to exercise and act on faith regardless and always; and yet, like us, they had no success guarantees, and no contracts which promised them the moon. They trusted God and lived and died by faith, many of them dying *before* seeing the outcome of their unfailing trust in God.

And these men of faith, though they trusted God and won his approval, none of them received all that God had promised them (Heb. 11:39, TLB).

So how did those great giants of the faith get to be giants? How did they exercise their spiritual bodies when the odds were so great against them? How did they accomplish those heavy works of faith? Why the same way we all do.

When those people were faced with life's myriad of situations, circumstances, problems, tragedies, crises, diseases and sins, to name a few—they were (again, like us) backed into the corner of denial and choice. They faced the same decision at this point, that we do. However, it seems that the people of faith, for the most part, refused to go the route of denial and went almost *blindly* for choice. And believe me my friend, that must have scared the daylights right out of them, just as it does us. After all, sometimes it's easier to deny the existence of our pain than it is to choose to seek a doctor, trust his judgement about the needed course of treatment, go into the hospital, and have the surgery. Those people in biblical times chose to act . . . scary as that was.

They chose, by faith, to become vulnerable. They chose, by faith, to make decisions and choices about their lives. Through their intangible and unseen faith they made what they *trusted* to be the right choice, based on what they *believed* would please God.

And lest you think, "Hey, for *them* it was no big deal . . . they were biblical saints . . . we're talking Enoch, Noah, Abraham and Moses here!" let me hasten to point out that those giants of the faith didn't *always* make great or even good decisions. I'm grateful to the Lord that he allowed the writers of the Scripture to reveal both the strengths and weaknesses of his chosen ones.

The Bible never disguises the fact that those wonderful heroes of faith were real people like us; and, while they are respected and beloved children of God, they did have their off days, *way* off days. They had their weak moments. I know they heard God, but at times, I believe, they didn't get all the message straight. Like a great many of ours, some of their choices were not so hot, and some were even sinful. We get carried euphorically away with recalling and retelling tales of their strong faith. One has only to read the stories of Abraham, Noah, David or Moses to catch the times when, I'll give them credit, they didn't shrink away from making decisions, but they made a number of choices which left a lot—a whole lot—to be desired.

This much can be said for them though, when those people came up against the time to deny reality or to make a choice, they, by faith, acted. Some of their choices, as I've said, were excellent, some poor, some misunderstood; and some choices brought sin into their lives. But these spiritually strong people of biblical times refused to sit on the coffins of denial, and by faith they got up and made their moves towards choice. They were willing to risk mistakes or to open themselves up as targets for their critics or enemies. And what moves me deeply is that neither God or his gift of faith left those dear people. No, instead, God urged them on.

And when—pray, tell me—when do we need our faith to be more overpoweringly vital and imperishable than at the time when the very choice we've made is inappropriate, wrong or sinful? I say, *never more than at that moment.*

For most of my life as a preacher's daughter, I've heard it said that sin kills our faith. But, if we believe that, I don't think we really understand the nature of faith very well. Faith's strongest, most beautiful trait is that instead of being strangled to death by sin, it comes more alive and carries us past the sin to the shore of sanctity and sanity.

In a manner of speaking, *faith* kills the power of sin. Faith doesn't condone our sins. We must also remember that the role faith plays in taking us *through* the sin of our lives doesn't justify sin in any way. Faith doesn't have the power, or God's permission, to forgive or pardon our sins. Judgment and forgiveness for sins rests in God's hands, through Christ's gift on the cross. And, of course, while our tendency toward sinning can and often does put a distance and a space between God and us, it is faith that bridges that gap in our estranged relationship with God.

Sin cannot kill our faith or even steal it away from us, and the reason sin can't do this is because, as the Bible states, *faith is a gift from God.* Tell me where it is written that when the biblical giants of the faith (or we present-day children of God) made a wrong choice that God, ever the good shepherd of his sheep, took back his gift of faith? Nowhere. In the scriptures do we find that God rescinded Abraham's faith because he lied about his wife, Sarah; or that God cancelled out Moses' faith after he murdered an Egyptian? No. God has a different solution for sin. He has forgiveness for sins—why else would the father send his only Son to die on the cross, if it were not to make a way of escape from our sins by his great love and his desire to make us his own?

And have we forgotten God's gift of Calvary and of the resurrection morning?

Faith . . . ah, faith's job is to carry us through. The reason I'm so emphatic about this is because four years ago, when I was hurling through that dark bottomless void, having made the most difficult decisions of my life (some choices—clearly wrong, some clearly right and others understandable only to the Lord who sees and knows all) it was God's gift of *faith* that was rushed to me and lifted me from the abysmal, emotional chaos of my life to higher ground. It was *faith* that whispered healing words to my dying hope. It was faith that stayed with me, refusing to pull away as if I had leprosy. It was faith that would not desert me and leave me to falling. It was faith that did not vanish into the wind, wavering and dying. Nor was Satan able to wrench faith away from me. *Faith came and stayed.*

Our heavenly father knows all about our choices and our works; and, in spite of them, he gives us faith. So faith comes to us, wonder of wonders! Faith never lets us forget that we, like the noble saints of Bible times, are precious, valuable, dear children of God. Keep in mind, it is faith that directs us and even carries us *back* to God. Faith brings us tenderly back to fellowship with God. It is faith that holds us together, tenaciously adhering to our souls like glue, keeping us steady on the course when we feel there's nothing left to us but little broken bits and pieces—incapable of being gathered much less held together.

My mother, because she was not the perfect saint, but, by her own description, "a weak unknown handmaiden," did not allow herself to go into denial about the gift of faith or the need of it's exercise. She knew her own fallibilities all too well, but she also understood the power and the wonder of the work of faith in a person's life.

In Mother's last letter, her simple handwritten statement to me to keep faith with God—*regardless and always,* was the expression of her desire for me to understand that this gift was more priceless than any gift she'd left me. I can hear her say, "Joyce-Honey, it's so important to know and have peace with God—but you will need to keep faith with him. Faith, Joyce-Honey, will take you through the darkest, most turbulent times. Faith, my daughter, will carry you to God when you cannot get there by yourself."

But this is not all I hear mother saying.

Over the phone, just a few days ago, my husband Francis read me a brief quote from Henri J. M. Nouwen's book, *The Road to Daylight* (Doubleday, N.Y., N.Y.). As he read to me, a strange thing happened. I could almost hear my mother's voice simultaneously reading along with Francis. The moments were indeed shimmering with God's presence. Listen with your heart to Nouwen's beautiful lines.

Jesus came to open my ears to another voice that says, "I am your God, I have molded you with my own hands, and I love what I have made. I love you with a love that has no limits . . . do not run away from me. Come back to me— not once, not twice, but *always* again.

All I could answer, in my soul, was, "Mother, you are right. Life's greatest gain, in the long run, is to know and have peace with God. . . . and, Mother, by faith I will keep *returning* to him. I will use the gift of faith. I will, dear Mother-Honey. I will keep faith with God—*regardless and always.*"

Chapter 6

Before I put down my pen and close off the pages of this book, let me say farewell for now, my dear friend, by sharing a few last thoughts.

You and I have been together all afternoon. We've walked, talked, and I've told you about a few of the gifts I received from the rich inheritance my mother left me. As I've poured out my heart on these pages, you've graciously done the listening. I know it sounds a bit one-sided, but that's the uniquely personal and intimate ambience which is created between readers and authors.

For now, our time of being together is waning and coming to closure. I'll finish writing this chapter, wrapping up my thoughts; you'll conclude your reading and put this book aside. We both, after all, must do things that need to be done. We must move on. We need to turn our attention and care to others, to other pressing matters, and give attention to our mission here on earth.

It is possible that someday we may meet each other in person, perhaps at a luncheon or at a meeting. We also may come together on the pages of another book, or on a spoken tape, a music tape or a video.

Before we go our separate ways, I want to take one more opportunity to confide to you the great riches and wonderful inheritance we *all* have as children of God.

Almost every day this week, I've come across another passage in the Bible which takes the wraps off our inheritance. I was thrilled to discover verse after verse dealing with God's riches and his generous heart towards us. In fact, the Bible treats the subject of inheritances with concrete and tantalizing promises. Take a look at the numerous scripture references to our inheritance in a Bible concordance. Humor me a bit longer, and read about the legacy which is ours.

The gifts my mother left me, that I've written about here and am now passing on to you, are not the Old Testament type of inheritance, as in land, livestock, or possessions, but more of the New Testaments kind, spiritual in nature—an inheritance for now and for eternity.

Read a few of these magnificent references:

Jew and Gentile are the same in this respect: they all have the same Lord who generously gives his *riches* to all those who ask him for them [italics mine]. Paul to the Romans (Rom 10:12 LB)

He that overcometh shall *inherit* all things; and I will be his God, and he shall be my son" (Rev. 21:7, KJV).

The Lord will open for you His *rich treasury*, the heavens to give rain upon your soul in its season, blessings to rest on all your enterprises (Deut. 28:12, *Modern Language*).

And now, I commit you to God and to the word of His grace, which is able to build you up and grant you the *inheritance* among all those made holy (Paul, in Acts 20:32, *Modern Language*).

We pray that you may be invigorated with complete power in accordance with His glorious strength, for the cheerful exercise of unlimited patience and perseverance, with thanksgiving to the Father, who has qualified you for your share in the *inheritance* of the saints in the light (Col. 1:11,12, *Modern Language*).

These scriptures, and many more, flood my mind today and beg to be written down. The words of St. Paul are extremely meaningful and touching to my heart because he was in the same kind of process of saying his farewells to people he loved as my mother was in the last weeks of her life. They were closing out the final chapters of their lives with loved ones and brothers and sisters in the family of God. Paul was seeing those people who were so dear to

163

him, perhaps for the last time, and it is evident that he decided that his words would be of hope and of their rich inheritance as joint heirs.

Think of it, we are in the same family with Paul, the other apostles, and the early Christians who have gone before us. We are, like them, children of God. The Lord is our heavenly father.

To some of you, the phrase "heavenly father" may not exactly compute in your heart or in your mind. You've nothing earthly to compare it to. Your relationship with your own dad is, or was, slightly less than wonderful, simply nonexistent, or downright pain filled and abusive. So, the idea of God being a father to you is not an altogether pleasant thought or an easily understood one. You have a hard time relating to and identifying with a "heavenly father" because of what you know and perceive your earthly father to be.

My mother had no such conflict. She was a privileged daughter. I say "privileged," because she was blessed by experiencing throughout her lifetime loving, warm and exceptionally close ties with both her parents. But, in particular with her father, because he was her only hearing parent.

When Marion, their first born, was still a young girl, it was her proud and loving father who took her to his barber shop and taught her to play a great game of pool and snooker on the tables in the back room. Later, after they became Christians and Marion dreamed of going to Africa as a missionary, and wanted to attend Bible College in Missouri, it was her parents who wholeheartedly supported her with loving approval and financial aid. Because of her mother's profound deafness, it was Marion's father who engaged her in many wonderful and spirited verbal discussions. The two of them forever talked about theological ideas, the scriptures and various concepts—right alongside the latest scores, facts and endless trivia about the much loved American sport of baseball. Long after I was grown I was fascinated by the sights and sounds of those colorful Hungarian duets of conversation.

When I ask myself how in the world Mother so implicitly trusted God, how she could so emphatically believe in him and why was she so convinced of God's love towards her—I have to wonder, how could I have been so dense? Her earthly relationships especially with her father, easily prepared the way for her to naturally perceive God as her heavenly father. She viewed God in the same manner as she saw her own father. Seeing, believing, and trusting the intent of God's heart was a natural outcome of the warm, loving, strong relationships she felt in her own home.

My mother knew of God what she knew about her dad: that both were alive and real, and that both loved her and wanted the best for her. Because of that solid kinship with her father, she understood better than many daughters of her generation, or mine for that matter, the incredible truth of that special verse in Hebrews. "He that cometh to God must believe that he is, and that he is a rewarder of them that diligently seek him (Heb. 11:6, KJV).

Because of her past experience, and by faith, mother believed that her heavenly father *is*. And by faith she believed that her heavenly father *is a generous rewarder*—a giver of gifts to his children. She also understood, quite well, that God, like her earthly father, did not take back the gifts of her inheritance. I was reminded of that by the heading on the church bulletin this past Sunday;

God's gifts
and His Call
are irrevocable.

I could almost hear the tone of mother's voice as it enveloped me and spoke to my heart,

"Be sure, Joyce-Honey, you remind yourself and others, dúring the times when discouragement makes you want to give up, and when you're feeling broken, useless and without hope that: *God is. He rewards us. And He does not take*

165

back what He has given. Your inheritance and your calling, those are still yours. They are yours to bind up the broken-hearted, they are yours to bring wholeness and joy to your own life and they are yours to give God all the praise, honor and glory!

Mother believed there were two inheritances. One right now for our earth-life and another, yet to come, when we stand before the throne of God to spend eternity with him and our family. I'm filled with a rush of joy because I know that, like any inheritance, the one that's been given for here and now is to spend and enjoy. And unlike a human legacy, no one can contest the will, or rob or cheat us out of what is rightly ours. There are not even IRS or State taxes to be paid for the gifts of our inheritance!

I could go on with this narration, but I will not didactically pound you with words about the inheritance we possess. I mean only to gently lift the conscious level of your understanding and to remind you, as a child of God, that you are his most precious heir.

I'm reluctant to leave you. I keep writing, maybe even redundantly, because we are friends, old friends, maybe new friends . . . but friends, nevertheless . . . and, bringing an end to this manuscript means a temporary "good-bye."

I don't like goodbyes, goodnights or farewells—no matter how bright the prospects are of our being reunited. I feel so intensely, in fact, that to even watch a family member drive out of our driveway after a visit, leaves me teary-eyed. Trying to catch a glimpse of loved ones as they turn the corner or board a plane, or watching them lying on a gurney, headed down a hospital corridor to surgery and saying *goodbye* has always brought a profound sense of sadness to my heart.

So it shouldn't be surprising that to end a book is, for me, like ending a visit, saying goodbye and wondering when, and if, we will see each other ever again. Somehow the feelings, which are flooding my soul right now, bring an urgency to my pen which makes me want to run after you, to catch hold of your shirt and say, "Please come back. Don't go!" . . . anything—just to keep us together for a little while longer.

I experienced these same feelings a few months ago. My daughter, Laurie—with a little help from her husband, Terry, and my dear husband, Francis—pulled off the best surprise I've had in a long time. Laurie flew in from California and showed up on our doorstep here in Texas to celebrate my birthday. We spent three heart-healing days together.

The only negative thing about her visit was that the hour of her departure zoomed in from nowhere, coming too soon. The awful feelings associated with farewells draped me with a sense of loss. As Francis and I took her to the airport for her return trip, I held up rather well. But, once at the boarding gate, Laurie's and my near-hysterical adieus and ruckus antics, especially as she was actually boarding the plane, were to say the least, out of hand and a bit ridiculous. I'm quite sure we embarrassed everybody, including the flight attendant, with the way we carried on. But our humorous routines were only a cover up for the gloominess of our hearts at saying even a temporary goodbye.

So, I have to ask myself: If you and I could catch or steal away a few more minutes, what would I want to communicate? What would seem most urgent? What line would I like to write at the bottom of this letter, as with my mother's, "Keep Faith with God—Regardless and Always"?

I guess, after having written about recognizing and receiving the inheritance that is ours—about using, enjoying and applying that inheritance—I would want to impress upon you the need for us all to pass along those beautiful gifts of humor, honesty, acceptance and faith. I believe it was said best by Norman Vincent Peale, when he wrote the line, *"Giving is living."* When we truly give of the essence of ourselves, releasing what is important to us, not just the tiny inconsequential things of our lives, but gifts of our talents, time, love, grace or mercy, we are talking about

167

touching the very heart-core of our personhood. "To give is to live;" hence, our inheritance must not be hoarded or stashed away in some safe deposit box but given away. It must be passed on to others and handed down from one generation to another.

I am certain that a number of you had a mother like mine or maybe the person most like my mother was your grandmother or your aunt. I can see you nodding your head in full agreement and in complete understanding—not only about a mother like mine, but about passing on the gifts that have been left us. You are like the beautiful and enthusiastic young woman who came up to me recently at a speaking engagement after I'd told about *The Inheritance*.

"I've got a mother like yours!" she joyously exclaimed. "Anytime you want to visit with your mother, come down to the part of Texas where I live, and I'll take you out to see my mother!" While we didn't have a chance to talk at length about her mother, I really didn't have to. I know that young woman (who has a twin mother to mine) is in the process of *using* her inheritance and *giving* it away—all at the same time.

Sadly though, in my mind's eye, I see some of you standing apart from those of us who had mothers like Marion Uzon Miller. You are pulling away from me, in the pages of this final chapter, and even, in some ways, from the world around you. You feel like retreating and withdrawing. Your head is moving "no, no!" from side to side, and in your eyes I see the dark shadow of disbelief and hopelessness. Your body language tells me you can't accept my words. And by the look of pain in your eyes, you wordlessly tell me that you not only did *not* have a mother—or anyone for that matter—like my mother; but, in reality, the mother you did have neglected, rejected, abused or just plain abandoned you.

I hear your hearts cry out almost in unison, as your grieved expressions mutely signal,

Joyce, I'm really happy for you. Your mother sounds absolutely wonderful. God, how I wish I'd had a mother like yours. I almost feel jealous because of your relationship with her. But I can hardly relate to a woman like that. I can't even begin to imagine what having a mother like Marion Miller would be like.

As warm as your mother was to you, mine was cold and remote. As caring and giving as your mother was to you, mine was indifferent to my needs and withheld everything from material necessities to emotional support from me.

I'm sorry, but my longstanding hurts are too vivid in my memory for me to forgive and forget, and my loneliness and grief over what I missed is too great to endure.

I don't *have* an inheritance of *anything*, except of pain and suffering and memories too hurtful to deal with. When you talk about realizing and enjoying our inheritance and then passing it on to others—I can only respond, "I'm sorry, but that's just not possible—in my life or in my lifetime."

My darling, wounded friend, one of the great pluses of having received these gifts is the fact that it doesn't matter *who* opens your heart and mind to your vast inheritance. It only matters that God, in whatever manner he chooses, tells you of your good fortune and discloses to you the warehouse which holds your priceless treasures. God gave those particular gifts to my mother, my mother gave them to me, and right this moment *I give them to you.*

Here. Take them. They are yours. Open up the secret vaults within your mind, unlock the dark, closed-off chambers of your emotions, unclench your jaw and fists—so that your fears and anger will relax a little, and give yourself a chance to become peaceful. On these pages, I've described my inheritance; and, since I am still of sound mind, I do hereby bequest these miraculous, God-sent gifts of my inheritance to you. They are now yours. Take ownership. Believe me, when I say,

> Your inheritance is here
> For you to enjoy.
> For you to use.
> For you to spend.

For you to invest
For you to become whole.
And in turn,
For you to share and give away.

Now I really must let you go, but before I do—let me tell you one last story.

My husband Francis and I accept engagements, going wherever we are asked. In traveling all over the country, we have talked personally, after the services, to literally thousands of people—for how many hours I can't count. And, because I have tried to be open and vulnerable with the message of my heart, as I have done here, it somehow frees people to come up after the meeting and share with both of us their most personal thoughts or reactions about the gifts of *their* inheritance.

It has been an awesome life-changing experience for us to listen to their stories. We have felt love's union with others and recovery within our own souls as we have hugged them, laughed about their unlaughable situations, or at times merely stood, holding them, weeping and whispering prayers into their ears. It's impossible to remember the names of each and every person who has stood in line, waiting to have a brief time of sharing with us, but those faces and their incredible stories will remain etched in my mind's memory forever.

One such unforgettable woman attended an evening banquet in a small Texas town. There were over four hundred women there and, after I spoke, about half of them lined up and waited for me to sign their books or just talk.

I first noticed her out of the corner of my eye as I was listening to the women in line and signing books. She was standing a few feet from me and, as far as I could tell, she wasn't *with* anyone. She seemed to stand clearly apart from the others. Then, it was as if my mind played a trick on me, because suddenly it looked like everyone around her disappeared for a second or two, and she became the only woman I could see. As she came closer and was almost next in line, I turned to get a better look at her . . . and my heart sank. I guessed, by the shortness and thinness of her hair and the color of her skin (or rather, the lack of color), that she had undoubtedly undergone chemotherapy and probably had cancer.

The next moment the women in the line moved on and there she stood, directly in front of me. Speaking rapidly and cryptically, as women do when they sense time is at a premium and quickly running out, I began with, "How are you?" It was not a greeting but a serious question.

"I've got cancer." She didn't hesitate or stumble over the word *cancer*.

"What kind?"

"It began in the ovaries, but now it's in the lymph glands . . ."

"You've had chemotherapy?"

"Yes."

I touched her hair and took her face in my hands. "How old are you?"

"Thirty-four."

I thought, *Dear God, my Laurie's age.* "What stage are you in?"

And with this she just gestured with her hand and shook her head negatively.

I said something about her time being very short. She nodded yes. Then we talked about how soon she'd be leaving, and I said, "Please, when you get to heaven, tell my mother I love her."

Again she nodded yes. She was holding up well, but I guessed it was costing her a great deal in strength and in courage. The women behind her in line were having a delightful time, laughing and talking amongst themselves. Their happy chattering was in such contrast to the pale young woman before me. I reached over, pulled her close and just held her. Then I felt her take a deep breath and heard her say how much she appreciated hearing about the inheritance my mother had left me, and how she'd waited in line to tell me about a decision she had made.

171

She told me a little about her wonderful eight-year-old son and, since she did not mention her husband or anyone else, I sensed that it was just her and the boy. She explained that her greatest fear in dying was the thought of being unable to leave anything to him.

The few unshed tears she had left within her rimmed her eyes, and she continued. "Up until tonight I felt I had nothing of value to give to him . . . no legacy, no inheritance at all. But as you shared the gifts your mother had left you, and as you gave them to all of us—I realized I *do* have an inheritance and I can pass it on to my son! I'm taking those gifts home with me to give to him."

We understood that this was the last bit of unfinished business she had to settle here on this earth and it was a tender moment for both of us. Then even though she was trembling, there was an aura of peace around her, and, when she spoke, her voice was steady with a quiet confidence. I held her a moment longer and whispered a prayer in her ear to our Lord—for her and her little son, and for both of them during the transition time between here and heaven's gates. Just before she left me, and I can't forget her face or the story in her eyes, she thanked me again for sharing the gifts of my inheritance from my mother, and for giving her the answer as to what she could leave as her own legacy for her son. Then she was gone.

My dear Mother-Honey,

Thank you for living such a real and beautiful life, for making me feel loved, for leaving me an enduring and precious inheritance, and thank you for this book.

Do you remember the prayer you wrote out to the Lord in your diary, when you were a twenty-two-year-old Bible College student? You asked God to make you fit, "at least somewhat" fit, to go out and tell others about the great "lover of our souls" who had so completely won your heart? And then, do you remember writing this to yourself?

Oh tongue of mine, if you ever speak, you must praise God. You must let your light shine for Jesus. You must

172

let your lips sing of His goodness, and you must let others see Jesus in you!"

Well, darling Mother-Honey, God made you fit indeed, and more than "somewhat"! You *did* speak and tell others about the lover of our souls. And believe me, not only your tongue, but your whole life spoke, and oh, so eloquently to everyone who knew you—but especially to your children. We heard you praising God. We saw your shining light for the Lord. We heard you sing songs about God's goodness and, truly, we did see the glorious face of Jesus in your dear and beautiful face.

I absolutely treasure the incredible legacy you left and I'm sharing those blessed gifts and memories with everyone I know as best I can.

Yes, sweet Mother, the inheritance continues to live on. You'd be pleased to see how alive and real those gifts are to all of us.

Before I close these pages, tell me, do you remember the last thing you always said as I left your hospital room? I do. Almost musically you'd call out, "Joyce-Honey, you are loved . . ." So until we see each other again, Mother-Honey, you are loved . . . and please know I'm keeping faith with God, regardless and always.

Lovingly your daughter,

Joyce-Honey

ABOUT THE AUTHOR

Joyce Landorf Heatherley is known nationwide as a uniquely gifted Christian communicator, able to convey Biblical principles with relevance, humor, compassion and gentle conviction—in a way that speaks to the needs of men and women from all backgrounds. A best selling author of both fiction and non-fiction (her 22 books include *BALCONY PEOPLE, SILENT SEPTEMBER, IRREGULAR PEOPLE, HE BEGAN WITH EVE, CHANGEPOINTS, UNWORLD PEOPLE, MOURNING SONG, JOSEPH,* and *MONDAY THROUGH SATURDAY*). She is also a popular speaker and conference leader. Recordings of her more popular talks, including *BALCONY PEOPLE, IRREGULAR PEOPLE, UNWORLD PEOPLE* and *THE INHERITANCE* are available on audio cassette, as are video tapes of *CHANGEPOINTS, IRREGULAR PEOPLE,* and *UNWORLD PEOPLE.* Her *HIS STUBBORN LOVE* film series, based on her nationally acclaimed seminars of the same name, was the recipient of the 1981 President's Award from the Christian Film Distributors Association.

Any speaking engagement requests or inquiries concerning Joyce Landorf Heatherley books and tapes may be directed to:

Balcony Publishing, Inc.
3011 Highway 620 North
Austin, Texas 78734